The
Supernatural
Murders

TRUE CRIME HISTORY SERIES

Twilight of Innocence: The Disappearance of Beverly Potts
James Jessen Badal

Tracks to Murder
Jonathan Goodman

Terrorism for Self-Glorification: The Herostratos Syndrome
Albert Borowitz

Ripperology: A Study of the World's First Serial Killer and a Literary Phenomenon
Robin Odell

The Good-bye Door: The Incredible True Story of America's First Female Serial Killer to Die in the Chair
Diana Britt Franklin

Murder on Several Occasions
Jonathan Goodman

The Murder of Mary Bean and Other Stories
Elizabeth A. De Wolfe

Lethal Witness: Sir Bernard Spilsbury, Honorary Pathologist
Andrew Rose

Murder of a Journalist: The True Story of the Death of Donald Ring Mellett
Thomas Crowl

Musical Mysteries: From Mozart to John Lennon
Albert Borowitz

The Adventuress: Murder, Blackmail, and Confidence Games in the Gilded Age
Virginia A. McConnell

Queen Victoria's Stalker: The Strange Case of the Boy Jones
Jan Bondeson

Born to Lose: Stanley B. Hoss and the Crime Spree That Gripped a Nation
James G. Hollock

Murder and Martial Justice: Spying, "Terrorism," and Retribution in Wartime America
Meredith Lentz Adams

The Christmas Murders: Classic True Crime Stories
Edited by Jonathan Goodman

The Supernatural Murders: Classic True Crime Stories
Edited by Jonathan Goodman

The Supernatural Murders

Classic True Crime Stories

Edited by
JONATHAN GOODMAN

The Kent State University Press
Kent, Ohio

Library of Congress Catalog Card Number 2011003224

ISBN 978-1-60635-083-6

Manufactured in the United States of America

Library of Congress Cataloging-in-Publication Data
The supernatural murders : classic true crime stories / edited
by Jonathan Goodman.
p. cm. — (True crime history series)
ISBN 978-1-60635-083-6 (pbk. : alk. paper)   1. Occultism—History.
2. Murder—History.   I. Goodman, Jonathan.
BF1439.S87 2011
364.152'3—dc22
2011003224

British Library Cataloging-in-Publication data are available.

15 14 13 12 11   5 4 3 2 1

For Jean Bloomfield,
'the weird lady,'
with love

Contents

Preface

ALBERT BOROWITZ

JONATHAN GOODMAN was determined to make The Supernatural Murders the spookiest of his true crime anthologies; he selected "accounts of killings . . . that were certainly or possibly sparked off by diverse beliefs about unearthly power on earth — or that were certainly or possibly brought to light by perhaps transcendent means — or that either gave rise to superstitions or legends, or acted as reminders, revivers, of old ones." It should be noted that Goodman, ordinarily one of the most precise of crime historians, sounds consistently a note of doubt or ambiguity. "Certainly or possibly," he suggests twice, and adds "perhaps," emphasizing the vagueness that is often at the very core of the supernatural.

If Goodman's introduction did not advise them otherwise, readers who are not already familiar with his other collections might be inclined to believe that his inclusion of thirteen articles in *The Supernatural Murders* was intended as a reference to one of our most popular superstitions. Goodman observes that his habit of choosing thirteen cases for each anthology was actually established much earlier in his career.

The Supernatural Murders begins with "A Slaying on Saint Valentine's Day," briefly relating the killing of a farm laborer, Charles Walton, on Valentine's Day 1945 in an area of Warwickshire famous for witchcraft. A celebrated detective, "Fabian of the Yard" (Detective Inspector, later Superintendent Robert Fabian), believed that a farmer, Albert Potter, killed Walton when pressed for payment of a debt and then embellished his crime with "counterfeit presentments of witchery."

In 1924 and 1925, a serial poisoner, Martha Wise, devastated the ranks of her family in rural Medina County, near Cleveland, Ohio. My article, "The Widow of Hardscrabble," quotes Wise as having told a reporter in a prison interview that her crimes were instigated by the devil. However, after her conviction, she blamed the poisoning scheme on her lover.

From the pages of Bram Stoker, author of *Dracula*, Goodman culls "Prophesies of Doom," an account of the murderous exploits of Madame Voisin in seventeenth-century France's Age of Arsenic. La Voisin's originality lay in her combining skills in two specialties: fortune-telling and toxicology. She developed an uncanny knack for predicting with accuracy the longevity of unwanted husbands, and for making her prognostications come true.

The discovery through a dream vision of the actual location of a corpse was a remarkable feature of the famous murder of Maria Marten in Polstead, England. However, since that case had been included in *The Country House Murders*, Goodman selected for the present volume Richard Whittington-Egan's "The Well and the Dream," a lesser-known example of the dreaming mind as sleuth. In 1922 Eric Tombe went missing. Night after night his sleeping mother saw her son's dead body lying at the bottom of a well, and she brought her fears to the sympathetic attention of Superintendent Francis Carlin, one of Scotland Yard's "Big Four." The police dug out disused wells at the burnt farmhouse of Eric Tombe's crooked partner, Ernest Dyer, and confirmed the accuracy of Mrs. Tombe's dreams by finding her son's body. Since Dyer had previously been killed in an arrest for an unrelated crime, the murder case remains unsolved. Goodman adds "An Astrological Postscript," by William Henry, who finds Dyer's guilt consistent with the planets.

One of America's most celebrated true crime writers of the twentieth century, Edmund Pearson, is represented by two short articles in contrasting moods. "Calling Madame Isherwood . . . " recalls a moment of priceless wit in a prosecutor's cross-examination of a practicing medium who had taken the stand, so she said, only after being authorized to do so by the spirit of a murder victim. "What kind of a spirit was it?" the prosecutor asked. "A plump spirit, above five feet high?" The argument of Pearson's second piece, "Defending the 'Witch-Burners,'" is advanced in earnest — that "we cannot afford to say much about the Salem witches if we chance to live where the custom of lynching Negroes, often innocent Negroes, is extenuated today." (Goodman appends Cotton Mather's account of the Salem witchcraft trial of Susanna Martin.)

Goodman contributes two excellent pieces to the collection. The first, "A Surfeit of Spirits," is his compilation of records and press clippings concerning an epidemic of ghost sightings in early nineteenth-century Hammersmith that terminated in a homicide. Francis Smith, in nocturnal pursuit of a reported spectre, shot to death the white-clad Thomas Milyard, who failed to respond when challenged. After he was convicted of murder, Smith's death sentence was commuted to a year's imprisonment. Goodman supplies a happy, though fictional, ending.

A second article by Goodman, "The Hand of God or Somebody," recalls hangings that went awry, including two failed attempts to execute John Lee. The hangman, James Berry, blamed deficient ironwork catches of the trapdoors, but nonconforming preachers sermonized that God had intervened to spare Lee. Jonathan Goodman offers still another hypothesis: "The 'Hand of God' theory seems less credible than a 'Hand of Satan' one."

In "Amityville Revisited" Jeffrey Bloomfield expresses outrage that the site of a real horror is now better known for the dubious account of subsequent visitations by poltergeists and demons. In December 1975, Ronnie DeFeo Jr. was sentenced to life imprisonment after conviction for murdering his parents and four siblings in the family's residence. Bloomfield notes that following the vacation of the haunted premises by the Lutzes, whose afflictions by evil spirits were detailed in *The Amityville Horror,* "the house has been inhabited by an apparently still-happy family." The new owner, James Cromarty, commented: "Nothing weird ever happened except for people coming by because of the book and the movie." On May 24, 2010, *Newsday* reported that the house was back on the market, listed at $1.15 million.

The art of William Roughead, master of Scottish crime history, is exemplified in the collection by his early gem, "The Ghost of Sergeant Davies." Set in desolate stretches of the Highlands after the Jacobite Rising of 1745, the murder of Davies was followed by a farcical trial in which hearsay testimony of the victim's ghost was admitted. Roughead notes that the Scots apparition spoke in Gaelic, "which would seem to be an appropriate medium of communication but for the fact that the soldier [Davies], an Englishman, while in the flesh had no knowledge of that tongue."

In a sensational French trial of 1956, Denise Labbé and her lover, Jacques Algarron, were sentenced to long prison terms after Denise drowned her little daughter Catherine in a vessel for washing clothes. In Rayner Heppenstall's brief commentary, "Devils in the Flesh," Satan's trace is omnipresent. Algarron was charged under a statute directed against those who by "machinations or culpable artifices . . . shall have provoked the act." Even a devil's disciple participated in the trial as Denise's counsel, Maître Maurice Garçon, a member of the Académie Française, who was an expert on demonology.

Lady Lucy Wingfield's letter to her daughter describing what Goodman calls "The Protracted Murder of Gregory Rasputin" testifies that the "Satanic Monk" had uncanny powers of magnetism and survival. Lady Wingfield relates that while Prince Felix Yousoupoff lay on a sofa meditating Rasputin's assassination, the monk was able to cause "streams of fire" to run through the prince's body. On the evening of his murder, Rasputin showed a superhuman resistance to poison and gunfire before his corpse was dumped into the River Neva.

The last entry in *The Supernatural Murders* is W. Teignmouth Shore's "The Gutteridge Murder," which recounts in an unadorned style the slaying of a police constable by car thieves Browne and Kennedy. This is a case in which I had never taken much interest until I read Jonathan Goodman's amusing postscript that associates the crime with a durable folk belief. It would be another crime to reveal more to the reader in advance.

Other books by Jonathan Goodman
published by The Kent State University Press

Bloody Versicles: The Rhymes of Crime
The Christmas Murders
Murder on Several Occasions
The Passing of Starr Faithfull
Tracks to Murder

Bumps in the Night

❧❧❧

I met Murder on the way —
He had a mask like Castlereagh:
Very smooth he looked, yet grim;
Seven bloodhounds followed him:

All were fat; and well they might
Be in admirable plight,
For one by one, and two by two,
He tossed them human hearts to chew.

THOUGH I DOUBT that Shelley intended supernatural
significance in those stanzas of *The Masque of Anarchy*, no
matter: they will, at least as nicely as any other sentence,
frame your mind for the following accounts of killings
(quite legal, some of them) that were certainly or possibly
sparked off by diverse beliefs about unearthly power on
earth — or that were certainly or possibly brought to light
by perhaps transcendent means — or that either gave rise
to superstitions or legends, or acted as reminders, revivers,
of old ones.

There are thirteen accounts. Anybody at once assuming
that that number was chosen especially for this collection,
simply because of the collection's title, is wrong. This is the
tenth volume of a series, and ever since the fourth volume,
each of them has contained thirteen accounts. (And at last
I have a cue to quote the good — is it anonymous? —
comment: 'There is no more brutal murder than the killing

1

of a fine theory with a hard fact.' And I can tell you something that a friend, Colin Dexter, has told me: that there is a word, 'triskaidekaphobia', for fear of the number thirteen. And I have an excuse for recalling Noel Coward's remark that although he was doggedly unsuperstitious, he drew the line at sleeping thirteen to a bed.)

Because of the sub-subject of this collection, almost all of the accounts in it *require* the reader to make assumptions 'based' on still slighter evidence than that misleading to the assumption I mentioned a moment ago – and, nearly always, those assumptions cannot be proved right or wrong; not even as definite maybes. Certain 'true'-crime writers – those who are prepared to concoct facts in aid of assumptions they made long before the facts – will no doubt sigh at the thought of how much easier, how principled, their writing lives would be if only all criminal cases allowed the assumptive licence of these.

The collection is not definitive. I'm not sure how incomplete it is; but I suppose that the most noticeable omission is The Murder of Maria Marten (said to have been brought to light, in the Red Barn at Polstead, by a dream), which is not here because I included an account of it in an earlier volume, *The Country House Murders*. If I had not also included in that collection an account of The Rose Harsent Murder Case at Peasenhall, not far from Polstead, I might, just might, have considered it for this one – on the tenuous ground of a legend (not unlike a tale told near the end of 'A Surfeit of Spirits', page 78) that, simply because the ambiguous Rose was cut down a little before, or during, or soon after a thunderstorm, every seven years ever since (no one can explain why seven), a thunderstorm breaks out over Peasenhall, though the weather is clement elsewhere in Suffolk.

Many callings have particular superstitions. (Why, I shouldn't be surprised if some 'exact' sciences have each gathered a sheepish few, though possible ill-effects of a pooh-poohing of them will be sighed aside as instances of Murphy's Law – or if even computer-dependent activities have collected some, possible ill-effects of a pooh-poohing of *them* of course reported acronymically: as MOUSES, perhaps, standing for Manifestations of Unbelievably Silly ErrorS.) I cannot tell whether the criminal calling still has as many superstitions as was once so — or, supposing that there *are* some, what they are, let alone whether they all have a pedigree or are a mixture of old and new ones. Only a day or so ago, when I was searching for an article, nothing to do with the supernatural, in volumes of a part-work, *Famous Crimes*, that was published circa 1902, I came across a filler headed 'Charms Criminals Carry'. (Serendipity, I know; and I know the saying that 'chance favours the prepared mind' — but fortuitous findings of that sort, not at all uncommon in my experience, can be viewed as evidence, nothing like proof, of what has been called 'the luring power of sympathetic magic'.) Here are extracts from the found — or finding — filler:

> Those who have made a study of criminals assure us that no body of people believe so much in Fate and its inscrutable decrees, as well as in the power of certain charms to alter destinies, as the habitual offenders.
>
> Many a burglar has been turned from the 'crib' which he intended to crack because a bat has flown past him while he was on the way to the scene of operations. Poachers frequently carry the small roots of one of the polypodia ferns which grow in the form of tiny hands, and are known among them as 'St John's Hands', believing that thereby they ensure success in their depredations and immunity from capture.
>
> From ancient times, peculiar powers have been ascribed to the mandrake, but it will probably be news to our readers to learn that to have a piece of this root in one's pocket is the first step towards becoming a skilful lock-picker, and should be possessed by all thieves who value their profession. The three-card-trick man and the thimble-rigger pin their faiths respectively on the dried heart of a bat and on a broken button, while the horse-stealer carries a small

3

piece of milt [the roe of a male fish], which is supposed to prevent the stolen animal from whinnying.

If you wish to make a criminal tell the truth, take care that he has no mistletoe leaves in his shoes, that he does not catch hold of one of his trouser buttons and twist it off, and that he does not double up his fist in his pocket, for though the latter may be merely a preparation for striking home his assertion, yet, in common with others, it is supposed to counteract the harms associated with a false oath. A more effectual method of evading the committing of perjury is for the deponent to place his left hand in exactly the opposite position to that occupied by his right hand when swearing, it being pretty generally believed that then the oath passes through the body without doing the individual any harm.

In times past, the liver of a child was supposed to confer invisibility, and as late as 1650 a child was murdered in order that its liver might be used for that purpose. Again, in old magicians' books we learn that to drink the blood of a human being, obtained by crime, is a certain cure for epilepsy, and, incredible as it may seem, the South of Europe can still produce cases where this cannibalistic remedy has been employed.

A belief in these same books led a couple of German soldiers to be charged with murder some three years ago. These learned 'magicians' had read that if a certain formula was repeated several times, a man's head could be cut off and put on again without him suffering the least in consequence. Furthermore, a man thus treated would have the power to find any treasures which might be hidden in the district in which he was. After a little persuasion, one of their comrades consented to submit to the operation, and after the spell had been repeated, his head was struck off with one blow of a sword. Alas! he went to look for treasurers in another world, and was quickly followed by his two companions.

Aptly at the end of the account of 'The First Trunk Murder' (of Celia Holloway by her husband John, a labourer on the Chain Pier at Brighton, in 1831) which appears in *The Seaside Murders*, a description of the hanging of Holloway, at Lewes, is followed by this description of a supposedly curative spin-off:

> Fifteen minutes or so after Holloway had been launched into eternity, a superstitious rustic from the village of Cowfold haggled with the hangman to have a wen, or cyst, on his forehead rubbed by the hanged man's hands; having agreed a price, the hangman escorted the afflicted man on to the scaffold, undid the manacles and placed Holloway's hands on the wen. He kept them there for some time, while the rustic knelt, eyes closed, lips moving, body trembling; then, really giving value for money, he untied the man's kerchief and thrust it inside Holloway's shirt, proximate to the stilled heart, and in one deft movement transferred the kerchief to the wen. The treatment over, the man descended the steps – not without some difficulty, for he was holding the kerchief to his forehead with one hand, searching his purse for the hangman's fee with the other. Two women spectators, both with wens, pled for similar Laying on of Hands, but their transactions with the hangman were curtailed by the under-sheriff, who, worried that his breakfast was getting cold, ordered them to take themselves and their wens elsewhere.
>
> The under-sheriff was understanding, though, about the hangman's traditional perk, and merely stood muttering impatiently while that worthy gave the rope that had hanged Holloway to a gentleman of Lewes in exchange for half-a-crown.

Whether the gentleman thought of the rope as a souvenir of the occasion or superstitiously, he seems to have got a bargain. Only two years before, in Edinburgh, the executioner of William Burke (lately the business partner of William Hare) had refused to accept less than half-a-crown for inch-long snippings of the rope, and, even so, had exhausted the supply before running out of prospective customers. I reckon, by a comparison of prices of like products and services, that the present purchasing power of an 1830ish half-crown would be at least ten pounds: still a lot to pay for a few yards of rope, and extravagantly expensive for a snipping – which darkens the mystery of why, so far as I know, none of the many purchased ropes or bits of rope remains extant.[1] Some, surely, were kept safe – perhaps coiled, if the length allowed, in a hat-box, or displayed in a glass globe intended to keep the dust off flower arrangements – and some of those have surely been handed down among heirlooms. Not that I want a specimen – but I should be glad if anybody owning a provenanced one could tell me so.

I intended to end this introduction with that request; but I have just received newspaper cuttings about a murder trial in California, the prosecutional basis of which strikes me as being quite as spectacularly 'spectral' as that of the witchcraft trials at Salem three centuries ago, and so I must continue a while longer.

The murder (if it *was* murder: there seems to be some doubt) was of a small girl whose body, dreadfully decomposed, was discovered in a wood more than twenty years ago. Only a year or so ago, a woman in her late twenties, a friend of the dead girl, happened to glance at her small daughter – and, simply from noticing something that appears to have escaped her notice before, that her daughter's eyes were the same colour as the dead girl's (the colour? – oh, that was, most peculiarly, blue), all of a sudden

---

1. Richard Whittington-Egan has reminded me that there is an apt passage in Osbert Sitwell's autobiography, *Left Hand, Right Hand!* (Macmillan, London, 1946) – that title chosen, Sitwell explains, 'because, according to the palmists, the lines of the left hand are incised inalterably at birth, while those of the right hand are modified by our actions and environment, and the life we lead'. He was born in 1892, and one gathers that he was about three when his mother, Lady Sitwell, allowed him, at set times on certain mornings, to wander unchaperoned around her room. He says that he 'recognised all the detail on the bed-side table' –

   but I did not understand one thing, a loop of thick rope, a foot or two long, twisted in a knot round the head of the bed.... Eventually, after many implorings, I was told what it was. 'It's a bit of a hangman's rope, darling. Nothing's so lucky! It cost eight pounds – they're very difficult to get now. Old Sir William got it for me.' ... And, suddenly, I was back in a world, instinctively comprehended, of Hogarth and Gay.

remembered something that had quite slipped her mind for two decades, *viz.* that she had seen her own father kill her friend, whereupon he, understandably indignant at her snooping, had said that he would kill her too if she breathed a word of what she had seen. She told someone, perhaps a policeman, what she said she remembered — and though there was not a spot of evidence against her father, he was arrested and sent for trial — at which, needless to say, the other star-witness for the prosecution was a psychiatrist. That person, having taken the oath that doesn't apply to 'expert' witnesses, who can be as opinionative as they or their hirers like, testified that the number-one star of the show had locked a horror deep in her subconscious as a 'traumatic response', otherwise known in the psychiatrical trade as 'repressed memory', till the sight of her daughter's eyes (sorry: her daughter's *blue* eyes) triggered recollection — and that testimony must have been swallowed by the twelve good men and women and true, for they returned a verdict of Guilty. (They had, I gather, unanimously pooh-poohed suggestions by the defence attorney that his client's daughter had ulterior motives for saying what she had said, one of those motives being a great hatred of her father, another being a great deal of money that, all being well for her so far as the verdict was concerned, she would receive from both a book publisher and a movie producer.) Her father is appealing against the conviction. For several sakes, among them that of the meaning of the word *evidence*, I hope, and I hope you do too, that the appeal succeeds — that the judge or judges of it will be as critical of those responsible for the prosecution and the conviction as American judges so often are of police officers who have failed to observe a nicety of arresting etiquette — for instance, by leaving out one or two of the 130 words of the mandatory Miranda Warning that a considerable number of arrested persons have learned by heart through repetitious hearing of it.

As it happens, the last story in this book is of the Gutteridge case, which I have included because of two widely-held beliefs — first, that one or both of the murderers of Constable Gutteridge shot him through the eyes because of a fear that a corpse's retinas retain, like a photographic image, a semblance of the final thing they saw, and second, that the fear was justified. There is a similarity, I trust you will agree, between those beliefs and the young-blue-eyes mumbo-jumbo. If the appeal in the Californian case is turned down, I shall, in any subsequent editions of this book, break with the thirteen-account tradition of the series, and make the collection up to fourteen with a horror story.

Jonathan Goodman
London, 1992

A Slaying on Saint Valentine's Day

IVAN BUTLER

ON SAINT VALENTINE'S DAY, 1945, as many people discussed the results of the Yalta peace-making Conference with tense interest (and perhaps more confidence than was justified by the outcome), at the foot of Meon Hill in Warwickshire an elderly jobbing farmer named Charles Walton, a native of the nearby village of Lower Quinton, was savagely slashed and pierced to death.

Mention the subject of English witchcraft, and the first particular response may be 'Ah, yes, the Pendle Forest covens' – they having been made famous by the colourful (and highly coloured) novel by Harrison Ainsworth, *The Lancashire Witches*. In fact, the cult was widely spread over the country during the 16th and 17th centuries; a long list of major trials recorded in contemporary pamphlets ranges from those of the Chelmsford Witches in 1566 to those of the Exeter Witches in 1682. Although cases associated with Warwickshire do not appear in that list, and although none of the local weird characters bore such memorable names as Old Chattox or Mother Demdike, the county was as notorious as any other for the scope of its black-magical practices – particularly in the district around Lower Quinton, a Tudor village lying between Stratford-upon-Avon and Chipping Campden (about a mile from the present-day A34).

Of Meon Hill itself, legend asserts that the Devil hurled a great clod of earth at the newly-completed Abbey at

Evesham, intending to bury it, but that Saint Egwin, Bishop of Worcester from 693 until 711, happened to see the missile approaching and, using the diversionary powers of prayer, swerved it to an undamaging landing-place, where it became known as Meon Hill. It was, so a story goes, haunted on New Year's Eves by a ghostly huntsman and his hell-hounds; but the origin of its name is disappointingly prosaic, deriving from a British river-name and probably related to the Gaulish 'moenus', or 'main'.

Long Compton, a short way south-west of Lower Quinton, was renowned for its witches. As a saying had it: 'There are enough witches in Long Compton to draw a load of hay up Long Compton Hill.' As late as 1875, a weak-minded young man, John Hayward, murdered a woman of eighty, Ann Turner, by pinning her to the ground with a *hay-fork* and then inflicting a cross-shaped wound on her throat with a *bill-hook*. He claimed that she had bewitched him, adding that Long Compton was full of witches, sixteen more of whom he would have killed if only he had had the chance of doing so.

Close to that witch-infested village, just across the border with Oxfordshire – and thus also within easy reach of Lower Quinton – are the famous Rollright Stones. In all probability, they are the remains of a Bronze Age place of worship. Legend has it, however, that they are the remains of a king and his army, turned to stone by an apparently well-meaning witch, to prevent him from conquering the Cotswolds. The story is that the king, determined to rule all England, met a witch on the high hill on which Little Rollright stands. She told him that if he could see Long Compton after taking seven steps forward, he would achieve his purpose. Confidently, for he knew that that village was close by, he strode forward – only to find his vision obscured by a tiny mound. The witch, cackling triumphantly after the manner of her kind, turned him and his army into stone, doomed to stay in the same place and in the same uncomfortably restricted condition until he *was* able to 'see' the village. (The legend further states that 'the man will never live who shall count the stones three times and each time find the number the same'.)

On the hilltops around Lower Quinton are other sites said to have been popular among witches. 'In the dark ages, the Quintons were overpopulated with witches,' one of the locals told Donald McCormick, the author of *Murder by Witchcraft*.[1] 'Today I reckon the population have overtaken 'em. But of course, a witch can hide in a crowd.'

It has been suggested that Shakespeare conjured up Macbeth's 'blasted heath' and its alfresco residents from his memories of this haunted countryside near his Stratford home.

I have said enough, I think, to show that the ground of this part of Warwickshire was fertile for the growth of rumours regarding the unnatural death of Charles Walton.

At seventy-four, he was one of the oldest inhabitants of Lower Quinton, where he had spent all his life. A sufferer from rheumatism, he dwelt in a thatched cottage with his spinster-niece Edith Walton. He was regarded as a 'loner'. In earlier years he had worked as a farm labourer, but as he grew old and less mobile, walking almost always with a stick, he did little more than trim hedges for local farmers, and then only when the weather was kind. Although or because his life-style was very modest, he was believed to be reasonably well off. Despite his lack of conventional sociability, he seems to have been generally regarded as a quiet and inoffensive, if at times short-tempered, old chap.

There were, however, eccentricities that caused some people to treat him with caution, even to surmise that he dabbled in wizardry. He claimed, for instance, to possess the power of communicating with birds and animals – and sometimes, if he had had one too many, went further than that, boasting that he understood animal 'languages'. He rarely joined his neighbours in a friendly drink at either of

1. John Long, London, 1968.

the local pubs, but was known to imbibe cider (considered by some to be 'witches' tipple'), having lugged barrels of the brew home in his wheelbarrow. On the whole, though, he was reckoned to be a harmless oddity; in his small community (numbering fewer than five hundred at the time), he seemed to have no enemies.

On the morning of that fatal Saint Valentine's Day (a day of rituals and superstitions, which chanced in that year of 1945 to be also Ash Wednesday), Walton took advantage of the sunny weather to set off to cut hedges bordering a farm belonging to a Mr Albert Potter, on a slope of Meon Hill about a mile away, taking with him his walking-stick, his hay-fork and his bill-hook – or slash-hook. His niece Edith also left the cottage, to go to a nearby factory where she worked on a wartime job. Her uncle told her that he would return at his usual time, four o'clock (she would not be back until about six), and would, as was his custom, prepare his own tea before resting from the day's labour.

When Edith entered the cottage that evening, she found it cold, dark – and empty. She called a neighbour, Harry Beasley, and they hurried along the dark lanes to see Mr Potter at his farmhouse, The Firs, and inform him that Charles Walton was missing. Potter appeared surprised; he told them that, around noon, he had seen Walton (or 'someone', he cautiously amended later) trimming hedges in a field about five hundred yards from the farmhouse. (An odd discrepancy was recorded on this point at the subsequent inquest. When asked why he thought the trimmer was Walton, Potter replied that, though he could not be sure, he was fairly certain because of the old man's shirt-sleeves. The coroner inquired, 'Have you been told that Walton had no shirt-sleeves?' A short-sleeved white shirt was then produced. Potter answered, 'I never saw the whole of him, only his shirt-sleeves,' and the coroner left it at that.)

Potter, Beasley and Edith set off by torchlight to the field in question. As they approached an old willow tree, Potter suddenly stopped and told Edith not to come any nearer.

Walton lay dead, spiked to the ground with his own hay-fork. Beasley took the distraught Edith home and then called on another neighbour, who got in touch with the police. Meanwhile, Potter was left alone with the body. His fingerprints were found afterwards on the handle of the hay-fork, but he explained this at the inquest by stating that he had tried to withdraw it from the body.

Later, Detective-Superintendent Robert Fabian, called in to head the murder investigation, described Walton's injuries as 'hideous ... [looking] like the kind of killing the Druids might have done in ghastly ceremony at full moon'. How familiar 'Fabian of the Yard' was with the sacrificial rituals of the Druids is open to question, but there is no doubt that the sight was horrific.[1]

The manner of Walton's death recalls, rather than Druidism, the practice of impaling a witch's corpse to the ground to prevent it from walking ... or flying.

The hay-fork had been plunged into the old man's body with such force that the prongs penetrated several inches into the ground; two burly police officers needed all their combined strength to extract it. In addition, a jagged cross-shaped wound had been cut into the chest and neck with the slash-hook, almost separating the head from the body. Perhaps indicating the fight Walton had put up, his walking-stick, saturated in blood, lay close by.

---

1. Druidism was the faith of the Celtic inhabitants of Ancient Gaul; the Druids were their priests. Though the name seems to have been derived from the word *dru* (meaning wise man — or magician), the priests were only very slightly, if at all, connected with what might be called conventional wizardry. Celts are thought to have arrived in Britain around 500 BC, but the only reference to Druids in this country in Roman history appears to be that in the Annals of Tacitus (AD 61): describing an invasion of the island of Anglesey by the Imperial Governor Suetonius, Tacitus writes of the islanders lining the shore in an armed mass, while 'close by stood Druids, raising their hands to heaven and screaming dreadful curses'. The Druids, firm believers in immortality, sought to placate the gods by sacrificing human beings. These were generally criminals, but when there was too great a fall in the crime-rate, use was made of innocent people. The usual method of sacrifice was to erect an enormous construction of tree-branches and twigs ('the Wicker Man'), fill it with humans and animals, and set the thing alight. Certain trees, such as the oak and the rowan (as well as the parasitic mistletoe), were sacred to the Druids: hence the superstition of 'touching wood'.

There was no apparent motive for the crime, and at the coroner's inquest the expected verdict was returned: Murder by Some Person, or Persons, Unknown. Walton was known not to have carried much money around with him; his old tin watch was missing, though its chain was attached to one of the pockets of his waistcoat. No one other than Potter claimed to have seen him out of doors on the day of the murder. What at first must have seemed to be a fairly simple case began to be complicated – chiefly because the locals, shocked or frightened, were chary of giving help to the police.

There was a suggestion that one of the thousand polyglot inmates of a prisoners-of-war camp near Long Compton was responsible, and Fabian investigated that possibility. An Italian prisoner had been seen trying to dab blood from his clothing while crouched in a ditch near the scene of the murder. With the missing watch in mind, Fabian sent a detachment of Royal Engineers trained in the use of metal-detectors to the ditch. The detectors click-click-clicked the presence of metal in the ground. Tensely, the police waited. A tin watch . . .? No – rabbit snares. The mystery was soon solved: the blood on the Italian's clothes was that of a rabbit – he was guilty only of the relatively minor misdeed of unlawfully leaving the camp to indulge in a spot of poaching. (But that solution raises another mystery: considering how difficult the Germans and Italians made it for *their* POWs to escape, how was it that the British allowed *theirs* to wander out of bounds, apparently much as they pleased?)

Most of the few opinions voiced in the village were conflicting. One farmer insisted that the killer must be a local man who knew just where Walton would be that afternoon – but another was just as sure that, in such a small community, someone must know something if the culprit lived in their midst, and so it stood to reason that he must have come from outside. An informant from Birmingham declared that survivors of an ancient 'black cult' lived in and around Lower Quinton – but muddied the declaration by adding that the murderer was from elsewhere ... and was actually a woman. In view of the violence of the crime, the idea that it was committed by a murder*ess* may seem improbable – but feminine strength, when stimulated and inflamed by frenzied fantasies or fanaticism, can undoubtedly be awesome.

While hints of local witchery were still floating around, the police conducted inquiries regarding infrequent, even 'one-off', visitors to the district, taking no fewer than four thousand statements from tinkers, gypsies, tramps, travelling salesmen, and even boot-repairers in Salisbury, in an effort to find the owner of some unusually-studded boots, the prints of which were found in the vicinity of Meon Hill. All was without result.

Of growing importance during this mundane activity was The Legend of the Big Black Dog. In a countryside so rife with esoteric mysteries and hints of the supernatural, tales of ghosts, warning visions, and sinister appearances formed, as it were, a layer of melodrama beneath the surface of prosaic reality. Shortly after the murder, the body of a black dog was found hanging from the branch of a tree not far from the murder site. Superintendent Alec Spooner of the Warwickshire CID told Fabian of a local legend.

In 1885, a ploughboy reported that on nine successive evenings when returning from work, he had come upon a black dog – which, on the last occasion, turned into a headless woman. The next day, his sister, hale and hearty till then, dropped dead. The boy's name was Charles Walton. In 1885, the murdered man was a boy – a ploughboy – aged fourteen....

Once when Fabian was on Meon Hill, a large black dog bounded past him and vanished from sight. Almost immediately, a farm-boy appeared. As he wrote later, Fabian asked him: 'Looking for that dog, son?'

The boy went pale. 'Dog, mister?'

'A black dog ...'

But before Fabian could say more, the boy 'stumbled off in his heavy earth-clogged boots'.

15

Soon afterwards, a police-car ran over a dog; and about the same time, a dead heifer was found in a ditch. Later, when Fabian was in one of the village pubs (named – improbable though it may seem – the Gay Dog), he mentioned his encounters on Meon Hill, and was told of 'a ghostly large dog with mad eyes' which was supposed to haunt the district: to see it meant death to the beholder. There is no evidence as to whether or not Fabian felt any discomfort at the thought of his possibly imminent decease, but from then on he – and his colleagues – received even less encouragement from the villagers. 'Cottage doors were shut in our faces,' he wrote, 'and even the most innocent witnesses seemed unable to meet our eyes. Some became ill after we spoke to them ... and one night, when we had waited all day to question one man who might have aided us, I said: "I'm inquiring about the late Charles Walton ..." He interrupted me gruffly: "He's been dead and buried a month now – what are you worrying about?" Then he shut his door. So we had to leave it.'

Shortly before his death in 1978, however, Fabian told crime historian Richard Whittington-Egan that he had long been convinced that he knew the murderer, but had been unable to voice his conviction in his memoirs[1] because the man was still alive and protected by the laws of libel.

According to Fabian, Albert Potter, who had died in 1964, was the only person who could have committed the crime.

Potter was the last man known to have seen Walton alive (and in the small, compact community, it seemed doubtful that any stranger could have approached the farm on Meon Hill without being noticed). In darkness alleviated only by the light of a torch, Potter was able to walk straight across the fields to the murder-site. His fingerprints were found on the handle of the hay-fork. His evidence at the inquest was both uncertain and unreliable. Firstly, there was the

1. *Fabian of the Yard*, (Jarrold, Norwich) 1955.

matter of the shirt-sleeves, which he claimed to have spotted (from a distance of more than a quarter of a mile) and by which he said he had recognised Walton, even though there were no shirt-sleeves to spot – or, at any rate, only short ones. Then he had contradicted himself when giving the order of his activities during the day – such as feeding his cattle and collecting a dead heifer (not the one I mentioned earlier) from a ditch. (The dying of two heifers in different ditches within a short while struck Fabian as being an odd coincidence – a fabricated hint of witchery?) Clearly, the coroner was not altogether happy with the answers of the chief witness. 'You cannot help us any further, can you?' he asked after a most frustrating interview. 'I'm afraid not,' said Potter, adding, with all the signs of earnest regret: 'I wish I could.'

Questioned as to whether he got on well with Walton, he said: 'I never had a row with any man in this country. I just let him get on with his job, and he told me what I owed him. I always trusted him' – which sounds like any politician's non-answer to a direct question.

Potter seems to have been a contradictory sort of person: sullen and unforthcoming, but a church sidesman (not an extraordinarily rare combination, perhaps); an active member of the British Legion, who could be abusive and violent when drunk, as he frequently was; an unsociable and shifty man, yet of seeming rectitude; a lover of cricket (which, in many opinions, would excuse almost anything) and horse-racing (which may partly explain the fact that he was often short of money).

Apropos of that last point, Potter was in financial straits at the time of the murder. According to Walton's niece Edith, he had borrowed 'considerable' sums of money from her uncle. It may be that Walton was pressing for repayments which Potter was unwilling, or unable, to make.

Considering all of the above, both Edith and Fabian were convinced of Potter's guilt. They believed that, when confronted with Walton's demands for repayment of the debts, he had killed him on the spur of the moment, and then embellished the crime with counterfeit presentments of witchery: cross-shaped wound in chest and neck, pinning to the ground with a hay-fork, dead heifers in ditches, a dead dog hanging from a tree....[1]

But the collection of pointers to Potter's guilt was not enough – not nearly enough – to justify his arrest. 'And so,' Fabian wrote in 1955, ten years after the murder, 'we had to leave it' – with the black clouds of fear and suspicion still hovering over the village of Lower Quinton. Fabian's last written words on the matter were these:

'In the offices of Warwick Constabulary, the case is not yet closed.'

In 1960, interest in the case was rekindled by the discovery of an old watch in what had been Charles Walton's garden. It was impossible to prove that the watch had belonged to him; any fingerprints would have been erased after so long a time in the soil. Even if it was indeed his watch, that could only mean that he had not had it with him on the day he died. What earthly – or, for that matter, unearthly – reason could the murderer have had for planting the thing in his victim's garden?

***

An earlier case of murder, which also gave rise to talk of witchcraft, was discovered in 1943, when some boys searching for birds' nests found a human skull and other bones, together with rotted clothing, in the hollow trunk of a decayed wych-elm in Hagley Wood, not far from Stourbridge in Worcestershire (and about thirty miles north-west of Lower Quinton). Other bones from the skeleton, and more bits of clothing, were found near the

---

1. With regard to the unnatural deaths of two far more illustrious persons, there are somewhat dubious theories that *actual* witchcraft underlay them but was *concealed*. Both Thomas à Becket and William Rufus (King William II) – so the theorists say – were leaders of covens; they were killed because of that, and the reason for their deaths falsified to conceal the unpleasant truth.

tree. As the result of exceptionally skilful work by forensic scientists and policemen, the skeleton was proved to be that of a woman about five feet tall and of slight build, who had probably been killed some time in 1941. The fact that a piece of the clothing was stuffed in the mouth of the skull suggested death by suffocation. The woman's identity was never established; a series of apparently-pointless messages chalked on walls in various West Midlands towns led to her being nicknamed 'Bella';[1] among any number of theories, the most daring was that she was a Dutch-born spy. The place of 'burial', in an old tree, raised the spectre of Druidism, with perhaps more justification than in the Lower Quinton case. But it is surely more probable that she was a stranger to the district (an itinerant prostitute?) who was taken to the lonely spot at the foot of the Clent Hills and killed after being robbed and/or raped – and that the criminal, acting practically rather than ritually, used the hollowed wych-elm as a kind of upright coffin, a convenient hiding-place for the signs of his sins.

---

1. EDITOR'S NOTE. In the spring of 1991, I gave a talk on 'the literature of crime' at the King Edward VI College, Stourbridge, and afterwards, during the discussion period, mentioned the 'wych-elm murder' in Hagley Wood, just down the road. Several members of the audience remembered seeing case-associated graffiti in the neighbourhood: most often, 'WHO PUT BELLA DOWN THE WYCH ELM?' or variations on that question. Subsequently, Anne Shiner, a sixth-former at the college, sent me cuttings about the case from local papers; also notes she had made, one saying that she had spoken to a relative who recalled seeing a chalked Bella-message on a wall in Stourbridge within the past five years. And Dr Alan Keightley, the master at the college who had arranged for me to give the talk there, sent me, among other things, a copy of a paperback, *Black Country Ghosts & Mysteries*, by – I swear – Aristotle Tump (Bugle Publications, Stourbridge, 1987). Unfortunately, though Mr Tump devotes practically half of the book to the Hagley Wood case, practically all of those pages are squandered on accounts of his searches for persons who, he hoped, could throw light on the case – but who, speaking of those he did trace, turned out to be unilluminating.

19

The Widow of Hardscrabble

ALBERT BOROWITZ

IN MARCH 1925, the supernatural was greatly in vogue among the citizens of Cleveland, Ohio. Harry Houdini had come to town to fight still another battle in his relentless campaign against fraudulent spiritualists. At noon on Friday the 13th, he staged an imitation of a seance at the Palace Theatre in Playhouse Square for a spellbound audience of 1500, including ministers of many of the city's churches. In the course of his impersonation of a fake medium, Houdini exposed a number of that shameless profession's most dazzling effects, including floating trumpets, strange voices, and baby hands that touched clergymen who volunteered to be tricked. Departing from the usual reticence of the prestidigitator, Houdini explained how he achieved an apparently magical phenomenon of spirit-writing by the simple device of having an accomplice substitute a slate with a chalked message.

To the right of its double-column-on-front-page account of the theatrical triumph of the 'world's greatest mystifier', the *Cleveland Press* published its first report of the hunt for a 'super-killer' in neighbouring Medina County. As news developments in the case broke at a dizzying pace in the succeeding weeks, the facts of the bizarre crime were to become shrouded in claims of diabolic influence that were ultimately tested, not by a Houdini, but by the common sense of an Ohio jury.

The first sign of trouble was a series of unexplained barn-burnings. The little rural Medina County community of

20

Hardscrabble, located near Valley City in Liverpool Township, about thirty miles southwest of Cleveland, was beset by trivial mysteries as well: disappearing jewellry and thefts of wheat and farm implements. It was the fires, though, that most severely disrupted the efforts of the predominantly German Lutheran farmers to wrest a living from the soil of their fields. The first blaze consumed the barn of Mother Gayer, and similar calamities befell Howard Grabbenstetter and Edward Bauer. Villagers whispered about the possibility of an arsonist in their midst; but when two years passed without any more emergencies for the local fire brigade, it seemed that peace had been restored to Hardscrabble.

In 1924 Medina County seemed to be caught up in the unremarkable rhythm of birth, marriage and death celebrated in Thornton Wilder's *Our Town*. On 16 December, in its regular column headed 'The Way of Life', the *Medina County Gazette* reported the passing of a woman who had attained the biblical age of three score and ten:

> HASEL. At Liverpool, on December 13, Mrs Sophie Hasel, aged 72 years, 13 months and 16 days. Funeral at Zion Lutheran Church, Dec 14, at 10 am. Burial at Hardscrabble Cemetery.

If Sophie Hasel's death appeared commonplace, her funeral proved to be unpleasantly out of the ordinary. After a reception at the Hasel home, five relatives took ill: Sophie's son Fred, his wife and their fourteen-year-old son Edwin, as well as Fred's brothers, Henry and Paul.

On New Year's Day, 1925, it was the turn of Sophie Hasel's brother, fifty-nine-year-old Fred Gienke, Sr, and his family to be stricken by a sudden malady. After eating a dinner of warmed-over pork, Fred, his fifty-two-year-old wife Lillie, and four of their six children, Marie (twenty-five), Fred, Jr (twenty-four), Rudolph (seventeen) and Walter (nine), became seriously ill. Lillie Gienke died on the morning of Sunday, 24 January; the hospital doctors

21

speculated about the possibility of a botulism, but the *Medina County Gazette* death-notice settled generically on 'ptomaine'. Lillie's body was laid to rest in Hardscrabble Cemetery, a few steps away from Sophie Hasel's fresh grave.

The strange illness attacked the entire surviving Gienke household again on 16 January. This time the two other children, Herman, who was twenty-one, and Richard, a year younger, were also afflicted, as well as Mrs Rose Adams, Lillie Gienke's sister, who was paying a condolence visit. The family physician, A.G. Appleby, of Valley City, two miles to the south, summoned the Medina County Health Commissioner, H.H. Biggs, who took blood specimens from each member of the family. Dr Biggs also dispatched to the Ohio state health department in Columbus samples of the well-water that the Gienkes used for drinking and cooking, and of the lard which had been used in the two meals that had sickened them. Provisionally, Dr Biggs ruled out the recurrence of a botulism, on the ground that the second illness of the Gienkes had come on too quickly after eating; an alternative theory of typhoid was excluded by the results of the blood-tests.

By 3 February Biggs was ready to calm the fears of the residents of Medina County that a dangerous epidemic was at work. He told the *Medina County Gazette* that another report from the state health authorities, focusing on the Gienkes' food, showed no evidence of toxic poisoning; the analysis of the household water was still awaited. Unfortunately, the comfort offered by Biggs was premature. On 6 February, a powerful third wave of illness swept the Gienke home: Fred Gienke, Sr, and his children Rudolph and Marie were taken to the hospital; a Cleveland nurse, Mrs Rose Kohli, who had been attending the Gienke family, was also stricken. Two days later, Fred Gienke died in the Elyria hospital, and a few days afterwards was buried beside his wife in the little cemetery on Myrtle Hill in Hardscrabble. According to the *Gazette* death-notice, the post-mortem examination of Mr Gienke's body had revealed 'nothing extraordinary'.

It was only on 13 March that *Gazette* readers learned that the facts of the investigation had been largely withheld from them. Under a screaming headline, **GIENKE FAMILY WERE POISONED**, the paper revealed that arsenic had been established as the cause of the deaths of Lillie and Fred Gienke and of the serious conditions of Rudolph, Marie and young Fred. Final confirmation of arsenical poisoning had been provided by analysis of blood and feces obtained from Marie and Rudolph; the Medina authorities now admitted that a post-mortem examination of the contents of Fred Gienke's inflamed stomach, previously reported to have been 'uneventful', had not yet been undertaken. According to county prosecuting attorney Joseph A. Seymour, the authorities had known for some time that the Gienkes had succumbed to arsenic but had kept that fact from the public 'in the hope that some clue could be discovered that would lead to information as to how the poison was administered'. Insisting that he had not yet targeted a suspect, Seymour would not even say whether the arsenic had been intentionally added to the Gienkes' food or drink. However, he ventured the opinion that the poison had been ingested in coffee, and revealed that he was holding part of the contents of a package of unbrewed coffee for analysis. While Seymour performed his demure fan-dance with the truth, the *Cleveland Press* was more outspoken, declaring that the medical findings had stimulated a 'hunt for a super-murderer who kills for the mere joy of killing'.

Significant progress in clearing up the mystery was reported in the *Gazette* of 17 March, although it remained obvious that full disclosure was hampered by the reticence of Medina officials. The coffee trail was still a major clue. Although the tests of the unused coffee had been negative, Fred Gienke, Jr, had observed that many relatives had become ill with abdominal pains and muscle-stiffening after drinking the beverage in his home and in the house of his grandmother Sophie Hasel – who was now for the first time identified as another murder-victim. Fred Jr had tried unsuccessfully to persuade the Medina officials and Cleveland chemists to analyse the Gienkes' blue-and-white coffee-pot, containing literal grounds that he had taken care to preserve. Despairing of the chances of interesting the investigators in his theory, he repossessed the pot and entrusted it to the city chemist of Elyria. 'I'm certain it was the coffee,' the young man maintained. 'I'll pay for the examination of this coffee and satisfy myself, at least, that the trouble was there.'

As Fred pressed his own inquiry, there was a report that the Medina police had uncovered the possible source of the arsenic. According to the *Gazette*, the scribbled name of a woman who knew the Gienke and Hasel families had been discovered in a druggist's registry; the name appeared again in the registry a week later, but then looked like 'the work of a person attempting to disguise his or her handwriting to conform to that of the person who first signed'. About two grains of arsenic were obtained through the first purchase, and one grain through the second. Prosecutor Joe Seymour commented cryptically that the 'finding of the registry had not been strengthened by his later investigations', and did not regard it as definitely established that the purchaser had acquired the poison for murderous purposes, especially since there was no apparent motive for poisoning the Gienke family: 'Administering of the poison appears at this time to have been accidental or the work of a moron. I have kept knowledge of the poisoning from the public in the hope of a tangible clue to run down, but those who have been investigating with me have found nothing to act upon.'

The prosecutor informed the *Gazette* that the only poison discovered in the Gienke house was a small amount of insecticide containing a toxic ingredient different from that detected in the blood-samples of Marie and Rudolph, who remained hospitalised in Elyria. Marie was unable to talk or turn her head; Fred Jr, despite the energy he displayed in his coffee-pot crusade, was still having difficulty moving about.

A Slaying on
Saint Valentine's Day

*Part of Lower Quinton, from the
tower of the church*

Charles Walton

Albert Potter

BODY WAS
FOUND HERE

*The wych-elm in
Hagley Wood*

The Widow of Hardscrabble

Martha Wise

The Medina County Court-House

The Well and the Dream

FRIDAY, SEPTEMBER 14

SURREY FARM MURDER.

THE MURDER OF MR. TOMBE.—Mr. Eric Gordon Tombe (left), the son of a clergyman residing at Sydenham, whose body was found in an old cesspool at The Welcomes, a farm in Hayes-rd., Kenley, Surrey, the owner of which, Ernest Dyer (centre), formerly in the Royal Engineers, shot himself last November.   On right: The police engaged yesterday in their search for clues.

THE WELCOMES YESTERDAY.—A special "Daily Mail" photograph of The Welcomes, where Mr. Tombe's body was found. Mr. Tombe was married, but had no children.

The *Cleveland Press* was less willing than the *Gazette* to accept Seymour's guarded account of the progress of the investigation. As early as 14 March, the *Press* headlined that a woman was sought as a poisoner of the Medina family; the slayer was 'a modern Borgia, who has so cunningly concealed her moves as to leave no single trace of her path of torture and death'. To the Cleveland journalists it was certain that the poison was administered 'at the instance of someone without the immediate family circle', and that for prosecutor Seymour it remained only to establish motive, means of administration, and 'a definite identification of the signatures in the poison book'. Two days later the *Press* had more to say about the mysterious murderer whose image it had begun to sketch for its readers: she was 'crazed by hallucinations growing out of certain deals in which the family of Fred Gienke figured'.

On 19 March, all the hints and guesses about a solution of the Hardscrabble poisonings ended with the stunning announcement that the murderess had confessed. She was Martha Wise, a forty-three-year-old widow of Hardscrabble, daughter of her first victim, Sophie Hasel, and niece of Lillie and Fred Gienke, the next to die of her poison. Allene Sumner, a reporter who was permitted to interview the gaunt widow in the Medina jail, wrote that the cold, bare cell was filled by 'the black breath of the dark ages when a horned personal devil roamed the world, urging men and women on to horrible crimes'. Crouched under her bedclothes, moaning and wailing, the widow 'pointed a bony finger at the vision of the devil whom she seemed to see standing in a corner of her cell', and held the Evil Spirit responsible for her actions:

'Why did he come to me? Me who always lived right and did my best, being weak-minded as I am.

'He came to me in my kitchen when I baked bread, and he said, "Do it."

'He came to me when I walked the fields in the cold damp night, trying to fight him off. He said, "Do it, nobody will know."

'He came to me when my children were around me. Everywhere I turned, I saw him, grinning and pointing and talking at me.

'I couldn't eat. I couldn't sleep. I only talked and listened to the devil as he walked through the fields of Hardscrabble.

'Then I did it.'

The *Cleveland Press* photographs of Martha Wise show a plain, long-faced woman with thick, dark hair pulled upwards from a square forehead, heavy brows above pouched, staring eyes, and a puffy, almost swollen, mouth. The prisoner told reporter Sumner that the devil had begun to pester her three years before, when her husband Albert, a farmer, died, leaving her 'alone in the house all day, with nothing around [her] but the wind and the rain and the awful stillness'. Repeatedly the widow asked Sumner to explain the infernal visitations, but the reporter, having no answer, left Mrs Wise 'shrieking at her devil in the corner'.

The poisoner's signed confession, published on the following day in the *Gazette*, was skimpier in its assertion of supernatural pressures, stating merely that the devil was in her. On the other hand, the factual circumstances of the Gienke poisonings were elaborated convincingly: on New Year's Eve, when Martha (whose cow had gone dry) had walked downhill to the Gienkes' to fill her bucket with milk, she had put some arsenic in the water-pail that the Gienkes kept in their kitchen for cooking and coffee-making; she had previously poisoned her mother's water-bucket on the day before the old lady (who had separate quarters in the house where Martha's brother Fred Hasel lived) took ill.

Martha had pinched more arsenic into the Gienkes' bucket either in late January or on the first of February. But it was not true, as had been suggested, that she had administered more poison to Marie Gienke during a visit to her hospital-room; instead, she had comforted her paralysed niece with a gift of oranges.

Mrs Wise had bought about two ounces of arsenic at a

corner-drugstore in Medina, telling the 'short, heavy-set man at the counter' that she wanted the poison to kill rats. Whenever she had set off to put the arsenic in her victims' buckets, she had carried the dose wrapped in a little piece of paper. Martha separately confessed to the mysterious fires and thefts that had plagued the Hardscrabble district. At first, she hadn't thought about the risk that the fires would kill anyone, but later she had started setting them at night so that she could 'surprise people'. She had never stayed at the scene of a fire, preferring to slip away to watch the farm buildings blaze, crackle and burn. She had set the first fire — to the Gayers' barn — after a son of Mother Gayer had shot one of her husband's pigs that had invaded the Gayers' garden.

Prosecutor Seymour opined that the arson confession 'virtually clinches the insanity case. The possibility of arraigning her on a murder charge is now so remote as to be almost wholly out of the question.' In view of the real danger that an insanity finding would diminish the exploitation value of the case, the *Cleveland Press* speedily staged a touching scene beneath the widow's jail-window: the four Wise children, Lester, Everett, Gertrude and Kenneth, whose ages ranged from fourteen to six, were shown waiting for a glimpse of their mother. 'She was the best ma any fellow ever had,' Lester was quoted as saying. 'The trouble with Ma is that she never did nothing but work with her young 'uns.' In a companion-article, however, the *Press* portrayed Mrs Wise as a woman morbidly attracted to death; she had loved funerals (especially those of her three victims) and on a recent occasion had travelled to Cleveland — on roads rendered almost impassable by soaking rains — to attend the burial of a distant relative; in addition, she had nursed her mother attentively after poisoning her. The *Press* had learned that the widow's attraction to death went hand-in-hand with disappointment in love. Her married life had not been happy, since her husband, 'pressed by his heavy duties in the care of the farm,' made her 'a slave to her chores and housework and children'. After Albert Wise's death, the family farm was sold under a court order to pay debts, and his widow had eked out the purchase of a small house only a quarter of a mile from the Gienkes. Soon Martha had scandalised Hardscrabble's proprieties by gathering men-friends. The Ladies' Aid of Zion Lutheran Church of Valley City, which had sent her compassionate gifts of flour, vegetables and clothing, had complained that she was redistributing the food among her male admirers. Local tongues had increased their velocity when the widow circulated rumours that she was going to marry Walter Johns, a Cleveland machinists' foreman in his fifties. When that project sputtered, Martha had proposed wedlock to another man, but 'was emphatically refused'. After those two instances of unrequited love, following years of her husband's coldness, the frustrated widow had turned to arsenic. So said the early reports – but subsequent versions added related grievances. According to the later embellishments, Sophie Hasel, and Fred and Lillie Gienke, Martha's uncle and aunt, had opposed her marriage to Johns, not so much because he was a decade older but because he was, of all things, a Roman Catholic.

The autopsy performed on the exhumed body of Lillie Gienke revealed a quantity of arsenic sufficient to kill three people; and, as Fred Gienke, Jr had suspected, the belated inspection of the coffee-pot disclosed the presence of the poison in scrapings of the outside metal surface, though the grounds appeared to be harmless.

The prosecution therefore decided to proceed against Mrs Wise for the murder of Lillie Gienke, leaving the prisoner's sanity as the sole issue.

Mrs Wise showed little interest in the legal proceedings that bound her over to the grand jury, and only twenty or so spectators turned out for the hearing in the extravagantly mansarded courthouse that dominates Medina's main square. Since no new sensations were produced in the court-room, the *Gazette* interviewed Coroner E.L. Crum, who had helped secure the confession. Crum got dangerously close to prejudicing the pending determination of Mrs Wise's legal responsibility by classifying her as a 'mental and moral imbecile whose normal side knew little of her subconscious acts,' and then explaining:

> This type usually displays a genius for evil. It is not surprising that she picked holidays – Thanksgiving and New Year's Day – to administer the poison. A flair for the dramatic would dictate that.

The coroner's observation that Mrs Wise favoured 'holiday killing' was acute, but he failed to notice the special opportunity that family reunions marking festive occasions provided to a woman bent on mass-murder.

In early April, the grand jury, as expected, indicted Mrs Wise for the murder of Lillie Gienke. The prisoner, who until recently had behaved calmly, now began to indulge in little 'tantrums', suspiciously as if she were laying the foundation for her insanity defence. Twice she had summoned Mrs Ethel Roshon, the jail matron and wife of the county sheriff, with a false alarm that she had swallowed a safety-pin.

In advance of the trial, set for 4 May, Martha Wise's relatives made the first effort to demonstrate the widow's mental incompetency by applying to the Medina probate court for the appointment of a guardian. The petition, signed by Merton G. Adams of Liverpool Township (husband of a sister of Albert Wise), stated that Martha had $1800 deposited in a Valley City bank, and 18 acres of land worth $1500. In the hearing, Mrs Wise stated that she 'did not know what she was doing'; and Joseph Pritchard, Mrs Wise's criminal defence lawyer from Cleveland, cited as evidence of the need for guardianship the conflicting instructions his client had given regarding use of her funds for the defence. Although the petition was not seriously opposed, premonitions of the coming battle over the prisoner's criminal responsibility could be heard. Dr Wood of Brunswick, the Wise family's physician, testified emphatically that Martha was not insane, while her attorney Pritchard still more emphatically rejoined that 'she is one of the craziest persons on the American continent'. Arthur D. Aylard, the president of the Medina Telephone Company, was appointed as the widow's guardian.

The murder trial began with arduous efforts to select open-minded jurors. Since many local residents had fixed views about the defendant's guilt, the court adjourned on Monday afternoon, 4 May, with two panels of prospective jurors (totalling seventy-four) exhausted, and only eleven tentatively seated. Mrs Wise, who attended in the company of the jail matron, Ethel Roshon, 'was dressed in a simple blue gingham gown, over it a heavy brown coat and with a simple, old-fashioned black hat. She appeared much pressed, but no different than on her former public appearances.'

On Wednesday, 6 May, when the jury selection was at last complete, the prosecution began to put on its case. By the afternoon, however, the courtroom proceedings were overshadowed by the tragic news that the Medina murders had indirectly claimed a fourth victim. Edith Hasel, the wife of Martha's brother Fred, had slashed her throat that morning in an outhouse near her Hardscrabble home. Ethel, who reportedly 'was never strong mentally', had brooded over the family deaths and 'imagined that people were pointing to her as the guilty person'. Apparently defence attorney Pritchard had intended to call Ethel Hasel as a witness, for evidentiary purposes that he never revealed, but quite possibly with a view to implanting a seed of doubt in the jury's mind as to whether the right family member was on trial.With the news of the suicide scurrying around the courthouse, the evidence offered by the state could not fail to be anticlimactic, particularly when the prosecution surprisingly declined to introduce Martha Wise's signed confession. Instead, Joe Seymour relied on the live testimony of Mrs Roshon, the sheriff's wife – to whom Martha had first admitted her guilt after her arrest at Fairview Hospital, where she was awaiting a minor operation on her arm.

The highlight of the state's brief presentation was the testimony of Marie and Rudolph Gienke concerning the effects of the poison they had taken and other incidents regarding their illness. Marie, recently released from the hospital, was brought into the packed courtroom on a cot, and prosecution counsel Arthur Van Epp (who was assisting Joe Seymour, his successor as Medina County prosecutor) had to hold up her hand so that she could take the oath; Rudolph needed to be supported by Sheriff Roshon as he entered. It was on the appearance of her two young victims that Martha Wise gave her first sign of emotion during the trial.

As the defence case opened, the spectators braced themselves for the parade of 139 witnesses whom Pritchard had subpoenaed to support the insanity plea. Martha's close relatives and neighbours portrayed her as a woman who could well have believed that the Devil had chosen her as his instrument. Emma Kleinknecht of Valley City, a sister, blamed Martha's disorder on a dog-bite she had suffered when she was fifteen: after this mishap, she had frothed at the mouth and her body was curved tautly backwards in the shape of a rainbow; she had believed that 'the gates of Heaven flew open to her' and that she conversed with angels while a cloud of white doves enveloped her. One day during the previous summer, a gentleman caller, encountering Martha lying on the floor of her house, with foaming mouth and glassy eyes, had deduced that her disability had not passed. Another witness swore that he had once heard her bark like a dog, and Emma Kleinknecht said that the widow used to roam the countryside at night.

At the beginning of Friday's session, Pritchard recalled Ethel Roshon in an attempt to emphasise irrational elements in the misdeeds confessed by the defendant. Mrs Roshon confirmed that Martha had admitted burning several barns and stealing a purse. The defence lawyer, however, lost more ground than he gained in focusing the jury's attention on the defendant's quarrel with Sophie Hasel: Mrs Roshon recalled Martha's having told her, in the intelligent manner she displayed in the entire course of her confession, that the dispute with her mother concerned the prospect of Martha's marrying a man of a different religious belief.

Martha's brother, Paul, remembered that as a child she was 'awful wild and had a temper'. To defend Paul against Emma, who had begun to beat him for some boyish misbehaviour, 'Martha flew at her and cleaned up on her. Emma had scars for a long time from where Martha scratched her face.' Many childhood friends remembered Martha as a slow learner who cried easily in school. Two of her arson victims testified charitably that Martha's husband had not been affectionate and had spoken abusively to her.

On Monday afternoon, 11 May, Pritchard called Martha's suitor, Walter Johns, to the stand. Although the prosecution speculated that Johns would deliver surprise testimony, Pritchard did not ask the Clevelander a single question. When Judge McClure rejected Pritchard's request to cross-examine Johns on the basis of his alleged hostility to Mrs Wise, the lawyer abruptly dismissed the witness and closed his case, although only about a third of the persons summoned by the defence had been heard.

In rebuttal of the insanity claim, the prosecution presented expert testimony on Tuesday morning. Dr H.H. Drysdale, a Cleveland psychiatrist, had a very straightforward explanation for the poisonings: 'She wanted to marry this man – whoever he is – and she took the poison-method to gain her end, which was to remove the obstacles that stood in front of her desires.' Dr Drysdale seemed to be speaking less as a man of science than as a spokesman for the Hardscrabble back-fence community – which gossiped, according to the *Gazette*, that 'Mrs Wise, rebuked by her mother for having men visitors, poisoned her, then set out to destroy Fred Gienke, Sr, because he admonished her after her mother's death'. Agreeing with Drysdale that the defendant was responsible for her actions, Dr Tierney, another Cleveland alienist, assured the jury that neither pyromania nor kleptomania was a form of insanity.

Dr Wood, the Wises' family-physician, rejected the defence hypothesis that Martha Wise was epileptic; he stressed her cunning, evidenced by her suggestion to him that Lillian Gienke had died of influenza. In his closing argument for the prosecution, Joe Seymour laid similar emphasis on the premeditation that was attached to the murder of three persons and the non-mortal poisoning of a baker's dozen:

> Slipping into the Gienke home when no one was watching, pinching arsenic into their water pail, returning twice to add further poison – that's not the manner in which insane people murder.

Still, the state asked that a verdict of Guilty be coupled with a recommendation of clemency.

Defence attorney Pritchard, in response, regretted that the jury had not been permitted to view the 'worn path' connecting the home of Mrs Wise with that of the Gienkes, a sight that would have dramatised the kindly feelings between the two families. He also condemned the authorities' use of a 'candy pail' to convey Lillian Gienke's stomach from Medina to the Elyria hospital for examination, without indicating that the sugary receptacle might have influenced the autopsy results. After expressing these introductory grievances, Pritchard evoked the forgiveness that Martha Wise's surviving victims showed for a relative who had lost the power to distinguish between right and wrong. Tearfully, he compared 'the condition of the ill-fated and physically-crippled Marie Gienke with the queer, mentally-unbalanced Martha Wise, broken in body and broken in mind'.

The jury of seven women and five men found Martha Wise guilty of murder in the first degree, with a recommendation of clemency, returning its verdict only one hour and ten minutes after retiring. The verdict automatically required the imposition of a sentence of life-imprisonment in the state reformatory for women, without possibility of parole.

Immediately after the conviction of Mrs Wise, Medina County authorities turned their attention to one of the men in her life, Walter Johns. On Sunday, 10 May, when the trial was in weekend recess, Lester Wise, Martha's fourteen-year-old son, had told Prosecutor Seymour that one day last November he had heard his mother discussing poison with a male visitor; when Mrs Wise observed that the boy was listening intently, she ordered him to leave the house. His mother's trial had already begun when Lester first reported the incident to his aunt, Mrs Merton Adams, who brought the boy to Seymour. 'I got out my old Bible,' she told the prosecutor, 'and Lester swore to me that he was telling the truth.'

On Friday evening, 15 May, Walter Johns was arrested in Cleveland on a warrant charging him with the murder of Mrs Sophie Hasel, and lodged in Medina County Jail. On the following Monday evening, he was confronted with Martha Wise, who now seemed anxious to shift the blame from Satan to her former admirer. 'He made me do it!' she shrieked when she first caught sight of Johns. 'He kept at me to do it! He told me I should get the arsenic and get rid of my mother and then I'd be free and happy.' When Johns protested that she was lying, she lifted her left hand – but then corrected the gesture, raising her right hand high. 'I swear it's true,' she asserted. 'He told me that with Mamma gone, I'd be more free.'

The widow backed her charges by claiming that Johns had asked her about a will Mrs Hasel had made before she was poisoned. Prodded by Seymour, she claimed that, without the influence of Johns, she would never have thought of killing her mother. Her lover instructed her 'how much arsenic to buy and how much to put in mother's water-pail – half a teaspoon'. Though she did not hate him, forgiveness was out of the question. She would have carried their secret to the grave, but 'it had to come out'; she was to be punished and wanted to be, but Johns was just as guilty.

While Martha Wise made her accusations about the poisonings, Johns denied everything she said, and so she changed her tactics, seeking his confirmation of the details of their romance. Johns, however, was almost as reluctant to concede their intimacy as to acknowledge a partnership in crime, and after he remained unresponsive to her description of the Gienkes' sufferings, her exasperation with her lover led to a new outburst: 'You couldn't shed a tear to save your soul from Hell!'

John F. Curry, a former Cleveland councilman, who was Walter Johns's attorney, complained that the widow's rancour was 'just a case of a woman scorned'. His client hadn't gone to see her after she was arrested for the simple reason that he thought a visit might make her feel worse; her false accusations were the result of his considerate restraint.

At length Prosecutor Seymour saw that Martha's ravings would not breach her lover's defences, and was constrained to play his final card, which was to demand Johns's explanation of a letter he had written to the widow when they were on better terms:

Dear Martha,

...Well, now, I suppose you are saying to yourself I guess I won't hear from that guy any more, but as usual, I have been very busy; it is a poor excuse I understand in this case, but you will excuse me once more, won't you, Martha; say yes....

I want to say to you that we have a very nice place to live in now, everything our own way and we realise how to take that comfort and enjoy it very much; I wish you could share with our comforts....

W. JOHNS

Seymour came down hard on the phrase 'everything our own way'. Didn't the words suggest that Johns and Mrs Wise had taken steps to clear away the obstacles to their marriage? In fact, the context of the letter plainly suggested a more innocent reading: the writer seemed to be referring

35

to the increased amenities that he and his children found in their new residence which they hoped the widow would share with them. Nevertheless, faced with Seymour's damning alternative interpretation, Johns appeared to panic. 'I never wrote anything about "now we have everything our own way," he insisted; the rest of the letter was in his handwriting, but someone must have inserted the disputed words.

Despite Johns's equivocal position regarding his letter, Seymour reluctantly concluded that there were insufficient grounds for prosecution and released the nervous machinist on Wednesday, 20 May. On the following Saturday, the convicted widow was taken to the Ohio State Reformatory for Women, in Marysville, to begin her sentence. During her journey — the first long automobile ride she had ever taken — she was accompanied by Sheriff Fred Roshon and his wife Ethel. During her two months of confinement in the Medina jail, Martha had made Mrs Roshon a confidante, speaking freely to her of the crimes — and remarking ominously on one occasion: 'It's a good thing you caught me when you did. . . . '

Thirty-seven years later, in 1962, the 'Poison Widow of Hardscrabble' was paroled after her first-degree murder sentence was commuted to second-degree by Governor DiSalle, and the head of the state's division of corrections announced that she would be moved to 'a home for the aged in southern Ohio'. Mrs Wise's freedom, however, was to be tantalisingly brief. Upon her release, Helen Nicholson, a parole officer, took her to board with Mrs Muriel Worthing in Blanchester, Clinton County. When they arrived, though, Mrs Worthing had changed her mind — 'fearful of a small town's reaction'. After this unexpected rebuff, Mrs Nicholson boarded Martha Wise for the night at her own home in Cincinnati. Next day, she returned her charge to prison after learning that the parole had been rescinded pending further study of its practicability.

Six years later, Martha Wise made her last appearance in public print. The *Cleveland Plain Dealer* described the famous prisoner's regime at Marysville. Because of her age (eighty-six), she was one of seven permanent patients in the reformatory hospital. For years she had worked in the poultry house, caring for chickens. Superintendent Martha Wheeler referred to her forename-sake as a 'sweet old lady', one of the best-liked inmates at Marysville.

Not all readers would have shed tears over the article: certainly not Rudolph Gienke, who throughout his life remained greatly disabled as the result of the paralysis caused by the arsenic poisoning. His sister Marie, also permanently handicapped, recovered sufficiently to marry and live to the age of eighty-one. She now lies at rest in Hardscrabble cemetery, where the Poison Widow dispatched many of her relatives before their time.

Afterword: Spring 1991

Martha Wise died in Marysville Reformatory exactly twenty years ago and was buried there. The details of her crimes are sharply etched in the memory of Walter Wolfe, an eighty-year-old township trustee and respected patriarch of Valley City, who recently escorted the author and his wife on a tour of the sites associated with the Hardscrabble murders. Walter is a descendant of the Gienkes – which is not surprising, he explained when he unlocked the gate of little Myrtle Hill Cemetery and showed us the victims' graves: 'In the 1920s, all the local farmers were "shirt-tail" relatives.' A schoolmate of Martha Wise's son Lester, Walter recalls his community's famed poisoner as a tall woman who used to walk 'cross-lots' from her hilltop residence to the Gienkes' place in the valley below. Both of those modest frame-houses still stand. Walter cannot account for the origin of the name 'Hardscrabble', because the land in northern Medina County, far from being hard to cultivate, let alone scrabbly, is rich; but the fair-haired wheat that was raised in Martha's time has now been replaced with less delectable crops such as soybeans and hay.

Prophesies of Doom

BRAM STOKER

IN PARIS, towards the end of the seventeenth century, a woman named Des Hayes Voisin, a widow who had taken up the business of a midwife, made herself notorious by the telling of fortunes. Such, at least, was the manifest occupation of the worthy lady, and as she did not flaunt herself unduly, her existence was rather a retired one. Few who did not seek her services knew of her existence, fewer still of her residence. The life of a professor of such mysteries as the doings of Fate – so-called – is prolonged and sweetened by seclusion. But there is always an 'underground' way of obtaining information for such as really desire it; and Madame Voisin, for all her evasive retirement, was always to be found when wanted – which means when she herself wanted to be found.

She was certainly a marvellous prophet, within a certain range of that occult art. Like all clever people, she fixed limitations for herself; which was wise of her, for to prophesy on behalf of everyone who may yearn for a raising of the curtain, be it of ever so small a corner, on all possible subjects, is to usurp the general functions of the Almighty. Wisely therefore, Madame Voisin became a specialist. Her subject was husbands; her chief theme, their longevity. Naturally, such women as were unsatisfied with the personality, circumstances, or fortunes of their partners, joined the mass of her clientele – a mass which, taking it by and large, maintained a strange exactness of dimensions. This did not much trouble the public, or even the body of her clients, for no one except Madame herself knew their numbers. It was certainly a strange thing how accurately Madame guessed, for she had seemingly no data to go on: the respective ages of the husbands were never taken into the confidence of the prophet. She took care to keep almost to herself the rare good fortune, in a sense, which attended her divination; for ever since the misfortune which had attended the late Marquise de Brinvilliers became public, the powers of the law had taken a quite unnecessary interest in the proceedings of all of her cult. Longevity is quite a one-sided arrangement of nature; we can only be sure of its accuracy when it is too late to help in its accomplishment. In such a game, there is only one throw of the dice, so that it behooves anyone who would wager successfully to be very sure that the chances are in his — or her — favour.

Madame Voisin's clients were generally in a hurry, and so were willing to take any little trouble or responsibility necessary to ensure success. They had two qualities which endear customers to those of La Voisin's trade; they were grateful and they were silent. That they were of cheery and hopeful spirit is shown by the fact that as a rule they married again soon after the dark cloud of bereavement had fallen on them. When the funeral baked meats have coldly furnished forth the marriage tables, it is better to remain as inconspicuous as possible; friends and onlookers will take notice — and when they notice, they will talk. Moreover, the new partner is often suspicious and apt to be a little jealous of his predecessor in title.

Thus, Madame Voisin being clever and discreet, and her clients being — or at any rate appearing to be — happy in their new relations and silent to the world at large, all went prosperously with the kindly-hearted prophet. No trouble arose as to testamentary dispositions. Men who are the subjects of prophecy usually have excellently drawn wills. This is especially the case with husbands who are no longer young. Young husbands are, as a rule, not made the subjects of prophecy.

Madame Voisin's great accuracy of prediction did not excite as much public admiration as it might have done if she or her clients had taken the public more into their confidence; but it was noted afterwards that in most cases the male individual who retired early from the scene was the senior partner in that congeries of three which has come to be known as 'the eternal triangle'. In later conversations, following the wake of the completed prophecy, confidences were exchanged as to the studies in certain matters of science in which Madame Voisin seemed to have attained a rare proficiency.

The late Mr Charles Peace, an adventurous if acquisitive spirit, worked alone during the long period of his professional existence, and with misleading safety. The illustrious French lady-prophet unwisely did not value this form of security, and so multiplied opportunities of failure. She followed an entirely opposite policy — one which, though it doubtless stood by her on many occasions, had a fatal weakness. In some ways, it may facilitate matters if one is one's own Providence: such a course temporarily avoids errors of miscalculation.

La Voisin, probably through some unfavourable or threatening experiences, saw the wisdom of associating the forces of prediction and accomplishment, and, with the readiness of an active personality, effected the junction. For this she was already fairly well equipped with experiences. Both as a wife and as a lover of warm and voluptuous nature, she understood something of the passions of humanity on both the female and the male side; and, being a woman, she knew perhaps better of the two the potency of feminine longing. This did not act so strongly in the lesser and more directly commercial, if less uncertain, phases of her art, such as finding lost property, divining the results of hazards, effecting immunity from danger, or preserving indefinitely the more pleasing qualities of youth. But in sterner matters, when the issue was of life or death, the masculine tendency towards recklessness kicked the beam. As a nurse in active touch with both medical and surgical wants, aims, and achievements, she was at ease in the larger risks of daily life. And after all, her own ambitions, aided by the compelling of her own natural demands for physical luxury, were quite independent, only seeking through exiguous means a way of achievement. In secret, she studied the mysteries of toxicology; and, probably by cautious experiment, satisfied herself of her proficiency in that little-known science. That she had other aims, more or less dependent on this or the feelings which its knowledge superinduced, can be satisfactorily guessed from some of her attendant labours, which declared themselves later.

After a time, La Voisin's vogue as a sorceress brought her into certain high society where freedom of action was unhampered by moral restraints. The very rich, the leaders of society and fashion, the unscrupulous whose ambitious efforts had been crowned with success of a kind, leaders of Court life, those in high military command, mistresses of royalty and high aristocracy – all became companions and clients in one or more of her mysterious arts. Amongst them were the Duchesse de Bouillon, the Comtesse de Soissons, Madame de Montespan, Olympe de Mancini, Marshal de Luxembourg, the Duc de Vendôme, Prince de Clermont-Lodève.

It was not altogether fashionable not to be in touch with Madame Voisin.

Undeterred by the lessons of history, La Voisin went on her way – forced, as is usual in such cases, by the circumstances which grow around the criminal and prove infinitely the stronger. She was at the height of her success when the public suspicion, followed by action, revealed the terrible crimes of the Marquise de Brinvilliers; and she was caught in the tail of the tempest thus created.

This case of Madame de Brinvilliers is a typical one of how a human being, goaded by passion and lured by opportunity, may fall swiftly from any estate. It is so closely in touch with that of Madame Voisin that the two have almost to be considered together. They began with the desire for dabbling in foreign mysteries. Three men – two Italians and one German, all men of some ability – were violent searchers for the mythical 'philosopher's stone' which was to fulfil the dream of the medieval alchemist by turning at will all things into gold. In the search, they all gravitated to Paris. There the usual thing happened: money ran short and foolish hoping had to be supplemented by crime. In the whirling world of the period, there was always a ready sale for means to an end, however nefarious either might be. The easy morality allowed opportunity for all means, with the result that there was an almost open dealing in poisons.

The soubriquet which stole into existence – it dared not proclaim itself – is a self-explanatory historical lesson. The *poudre de succession*[1] marks an epoch which, for sheer, regardless, remorseless, profligate wickedness is almost without peer in history (and this is said without forgetting the time of the Borgias). Not even natural affection or family life or individual relationship or friendliness was afforded any consideration. This phase of crime, which was almost confined to the upper and wealthier classes, depended on wealth and laws of heredity and entail. Those who benefited by it salved what remnants of conscience still remained to them with the thought that they were simply helping the natural process of waste and recuperation. The old and feeble were removed, with as little fuss as might be necessary, in order that the young and lusty might benefit. As the change was a form of plunder, which had to be paid for in a degree in some way approximate to results, prices ran high. Poisoning on a successful scale requires skilful and daring agents, whose after-secrecy as well as whose present aid has to be secured. Exili and Glasser – one of the Italians and the German – did a thriving trade. As usual in such illicit traffic, the possibility of purchase under effective conditions made a

---

1. *Poudre* here means 'poison'; and the whole phrase can be read colloquially – 'the too general use of poison as a safe means of getting superfluous people permanently out of the way'.

market. There is every reason to believe from after-results that La Voisin was one such agent. The cause of La Brinvilliers entering the market was the purely personal one of an affair of sensual passion.

Death is an informative circumstance. Suspicion began to leak out that the polyglot firm of needy foreigners had dark dealings. Two of them – the Italians – were arrested and sent to the Bastille, where one of them died. By unhappy chance, the other was given as a cell-companion Captain Sainte-Croix, who was a lover of the Marquise de Brinvilliers. Sainte-Croix, as a Captain in the regiment of the Marquis, had become intimate in his house. Brinvilliers was a fatuous person and of imperfect moral vision. The Captain was handsome, and Madame la Marquise amorous. Behold, then, the usual personnel of a tragedy of three. After a while, the intrigue became a matter of family concern. The lady's father, the Civil Lieutenant d'Aulroy, procured a *lettre de cachet* (Royal warrant), and had the erring lover immured in the Bastille as the easiest and least public way out of the difficulty. 'Evil communications corrupt good manners,' says the proverb. The proverbial philosopher understated the danger of such juxtaposition. Evil manners add corruption even to their kind. In the Bastille, the exasperated lover listened to the wiles of Exili; and another stage of misdoing began. The Marquise determined on revenge, and be sure that in such a period even the massive walls of the Bastille could not prevent the secret whisper of a means of effecting it. D'Aulroy, his two sons, and another sister perished. Brinvilliers himself was spared through some bizarre freak of his wife's conscience. Then the secret began to be whispered – first, it was said, through the confessional – and the *Chambre Ardente* (analogous to the Star Chamber), instituted for such purposes, took the case in hand. The result might have been doubtful, for great social forces were at work to hush up such a scandal, but for the fact that, with a truly seventeenth-century candour, the Marquise had written an elaborate confession of her guilt, which if it did not directly assure condemnation, at least put justice on the right track.

The trial was a celebrated one, and involved incidentally many illustrious persons as well as others of lesser note. In the end, in 1676, Madame la Marquise de Brinvilliers was burned – that is, what was left of her was burned after her head had been cut off: a matter of grace in consideration of her rank. It was soothing to the feelings of many relatives and friends – not to mention those of the principal – in such a case, when 'great command o'erswayed the order' of purgation by fire.

Before the eddy of the Brinvilliers' criminal scandal reached to the lower level of Madame Voisin, a good many scandals were aired; though again 'great command' seems to have been operative, so far as human power availed, in minimising both scandals and punishments. Amongst those cited to the *Chambre Ardente* were two nieces of Cardinal Mazarin, the Duchesse de Bouillon, the Comtesse de Soissons, and Marshal de Luxembourg. In some of these cases, that which in theatrical parlance is called 'comic relief' was not wanting. It was a witty if impertinent answer of the Duchesse de Bouillon to one of her judges, La Reyne, an ill-favoured man, who asked, apropos of a statement made at the trial that she had taken part in an alleged invocation of Beelzebub, 'and did you ever see the Devil?' – 'Yes, I am looking at him now. He is ugly, and is disguised as a Councillor of State!'

The King, Louis XIV, took much interest in the trial and even tried now and again to smooth matters. He went so far as to advise the Comtesse de Soissons, who was treated rather as a foolish than as a guilty woman, to keep out of the way if she were really guilty. In answer, she said with the haughtiness of her time that, though she was innocent, she did not care to appear in a Law Court. She withdrew to Brussels, where she died some twenty years later. Marshal de Luxembourg – François Henri de Montmorenci-Boutteville, duke, peer, Marshal of France, to give his full titles – was shown to have engaged in an attempt to recover lost property by occult means. On that basis, and because he had once asked Madame Voisin to produce His Satanic Majesty, he was alleged to have sold himself to the Devil. But his occult adventures did not stand in the way of his promotion as a soldier, though he had to stand a trial of over a year long: he was made Captain of the Guard and finally given command of the Army.

La Voisin and her accomplices – a woman named Vigoureux, and Le Sage, a priest – were with a couple of score of others arrested in 1679, and, after a spell of imprisonment in the Bastille, tried. As a result, Voisin, Vigoureux and her brother, and Le Sage were burned early in 1680. In Voisin's case, the mercy of previous decapitation, which had been accorded to her guilty sister Brinvilliers, was not granted. Perhaps this was partly because of the attitude she had taken with regard to religious matters. Amongst other unforgivable acts, she had repelled the Crucifix – a terrible thing to do, according to the ideas of that superstitious age.

The Well and the Dream

RICHARD WHITTINGTON-EGAN

Between the acting of a dreadful thing
And the first motion, all the interim is
Like a phantasma, or a hideous dream.

Wordsworth: *In Memoriam*

HURRICANE-LAMPS FLICKERED like Will-o'-the-wisps among the tall, rank grasses and clutching tangles of weeds on the deserted farm. Their thin yellow beams chased shadows through the overhanging branches, and shone on the bared arms of the searchers, that September midnight.

Shortly before sundown, they had slipped like a marauding band of body-snatchers through the five-barred gate in Hayes Lane, at Kenley, near Croydon, on the south-eastern outskirts of London, to begin their grim and secret hunt at The Welcomes Farm.

For nearly six hours they had been picking and shovelling the rubble of tight-packed earth, crumbling bricks and concrete from two of the farm's five wells.

Now they were working on the third....

It was a strange story which had brought Superintendent Francis Carlin, one of the 'Big Four' of Scotland Yard, and his men to the lonely farm that night. A story which Carlin was afterwards to describe as the most extraordinary in all his thirty-five years' experience.

It had really begun years before – in 1919. The Great War, which had scythed through 'the flower of England's youth', had ended. The survivors were taking up – or trying to – the threads of peacetime life. Among them were two demobilised Army officers, twenty-five-year-old Eric Gordon-Tombe and twenty-seven-year-old Ernest Dyer.

They had been lucky. In the 'land fit for heroes to live in' other young ex-officers were selling boot-laces, but these two had landed respectable jobs at the Air Ministry in London.

Lucky? Their chance-ordained meeting was to spell disaster for both of them.

Someone who knew them at this time was a young ex-gunner officer now helping in his father's wine business in the Haymarket. His name was Dennis Wheatley. Still fourteen years away from publishing the first of the novels that were to make him the widely acknowledged 'Prince of Storytellers', he could not have guessed that these two young men were to act out a real-life mystery as bizarre as any tale ever to come from his imaginative pen.

He told me: 'I met young Tombe in a camp for convalescent officers in the spring of 1917. We shared a hut together for several months. I resumed my friendship with him after I was invalided back from France. Dyer I met only a few times, but there was something about him I didn't like.'

Dyer had big schemes. Motoring and horse-racing, he said, signposted the road to great fortunes. Tombe had £3000 in the bank. They decided to go into partnership.

Two motor businesses were started – at Harlesden, north London, and in Westminster Bridge Road. Both failed. The partners then purchased a race-horse training stable and stud farm – The Welcomes – Tombe putting up the greater part of the money. That was in 1920.

Dyer, his wife Annie, and their three children lived in the farmhouse. Tombe stayed either at his flat in the Haymarket or, less often, at a hotel in Dorking, ten miles or so south-west of Kenley.

Shortly before nine o'clock each morning, he would arrive at Kenley Railway Station, where he would be met by a pony and trap, and driven to The Welcomes. He would spend the day there, and be driven back to the station at about six o'clock.

Then, one night in April 1921, the farmhouse burnt down. Dyer, with his wife and children, moved in over the stables – and he also moved in with a swift claim against the insurance company.

The place had cost £5000. Dyer had insured it for £12,000. Suspicious after a sharp-eyed insurance inspector had spotted a number of petrol tins, the company declined to settle. And Dyer was shrewd enough not to press his claim.

After the fire, no more business was conducted at the farm, and Dyer was beginning to cast around for ready cash. His tanglings with fast women and slow horses were proving expensive. He needed money. At first he obtained it by borrowing from Tombe. Then he forged his partner's name on several cheques. Discovery, accusations and a bitter quarrel followed.

The new year – 1922 – started badly. Three months went by without much improvement. Then Tombe simply vanished from the face of the earth. The last trace that anyone had of him was a letter. Addressed to his parents, it was dated Tuesday, 17 April. 'I shall be coming to see you on Saturday,' it said.

Eric Tombe never arrived.

In their little house in Wells Road, Sydenham (seven miles north of Kenley), the Reverend George Gordon-Tombe and his wife watched for the postman, listened for the doorbell, waited for some word of their son. The weeks lengthened into months. Puzzled, plagued with anxiety, the frail, sixty-year-old, retired clergyman turned detective. He began putting advertisements in the personal columns of the papers. No reply. He spent three months scouring the West End for clues. Drew blank after blank. Just as he was starting to despair of ever finding out anything, his luck changed.

'I went to see a barber, Mr Richards of the Haymarket, to ask if he had seen my son lately. He told me no, not for a long time. But as I was leaving the shop, a thought struck me to ask if Eric had ever brought any friends there. The barber kept a little book in which he recorded any introductions by his customers. In it was written: 'Ernest Dyer, The Welcomes, Kenley. Introduced by Mr Eric Tombe.'

The name Dyer meant nothing to the retired clergyman, but he lost no time in paying a visit to The Welcomes. Dyer was not there, but his wife was. She could tell him nothing definite, but was able to give him an address in Yorkshire where, she said, a close friend of his son's lived. Mr Tombe left at once for Yorkshire.

There he heard a tale that seemed to confirm his worst fears. The daughter of the house said that she had last seen Eric in March 1922. He had arranged to meet her and another young woman, to whom he was engaged, at Euston Station on 25 April. Dyer was to meet them there, too, and the four of them were to take a brief trip to Paris. When they arrived at Euston, however, Dyer was on his own. He showed them a telegram which he said had come from Eric – 'SORRY TO DISAPPOINT. HAVE BEEN CALLED OVERSEAS.'

That word 'overseas' had aroused one of the girls' suspicions. 'It wasn't one of Eric's expressions,' she said. 'He never used it. But Dyer did.' And she told Dyer point-blank, 'I don't believe that telegram is genuine. I think you've made away with Eric, and I shall go straight to Scotland Yard.' Dyer became very agitated. 'Don't do that,' he pleaded. 'If you do, I shall blow my brains out.'

The Paris trip was called off.

Thoroughly alarmed now, Mr Tombe caught the next train back to London, where he went to see the manager of his son's bank. 'I don't think you need to worry,' the manager told him. 'We have a letter here which was written by your son only last month.'

The letter was dated 22 July 1922. Mr Tombe scrutinised it closely.

'That is not my son's signature,' he said. 'This letter is a forgery.'

The manager's turn to look worried. Rapidly he leafed through Eric Tombe's file.

April 1922	Credit balance £2570. Letter from Tombe requesting transfer of £1350 to the Paris branch, and asking that his partner, Ernest Dyer, be allowed to draw on it.
July 1922	Letter from Tombe notifying that he had given power of attorney to Ernest Dyer.
August 1922	Tombe's account substantially overdrawn.

When Mr Tombe left the bank, he was absolutely convinced that Ernest Dyer was not only a forger and a thief — but also a murderer.

But where was Ernest Dyer? His wife didn't know. He had not been seen at The Welcomes for months. He had vanished as totally and mysteriously as Eric Tombe.

The time Three months later. 16 November 1922.
The place The Yorkshire seaside town of Scarborough.

Mr James Fitzsimmons is just finishing his lunch in the dining-room of the Old Bar Hotel when he receives a message that there is a gentleman asking to see him.

The gentleman is Detective Inspector Abbott of the Scarborough CID, and he is anxious to ask Mr Fitzsimmons a few questions regarding a number of dud cheques which he has been passing. He is also requiring an explanation concerning an advertisement which Mr Fitzsimmons has inserted in the local papers, inviting men 'of the highest integrity' to contact him with a view to obtaining employment with exceptionally good prospects. All they had to do was to produce a substantial cash deposit to establish their probity. It was one of the oldest tricks in the confidence business.

Mr Fitzsimmons is all charm and plausibility. 'Of course, of course, Inspector. Now, if you will just step upstairs to my room, I'm sure we can clear this matter up to your entire satisfaction.'

It was as they reached the landing that Abbott saw Fitzsimmons make a suspicious movement towards his pocket. Thinking that he was about to destroy some incriminating evidence, Abbott seized hold of him.

There was a struggle. The two men crashed to the ground. A flash ... an ear-splitting explosion. Fitzsimmons went limp. The bullet from the revolver he had pulled from his pocket had killed him instantly.

Later, when the police searched Fitzsimmons's room, they discovered a suitcase bearing the initials 'E.T.'. They found, too, a passport in the name of Eric Gordon-Tombe – and 180 cheque forms, on each of which was pencilled Tombe's forged signature.

James Fitzsimmons was Ernest Dyer.

But where was Eric Tombe?

Dyer had been dead and buried ten months on the day that the Reverend George Gordon-Tombe called at Scotland Yard.

Superintendent Carlin sat at his big desk and listened politely to the incredible story that the clergyman was telling him of his wife's recurrent nightmare. Night after night, he said, Mrs Tombe had had the same terrifying dream. In it, she saw her son's dead body lying at the foot of a well.

Carlin was sympathetic – but dubious. Dreams are not evidence in the matter-of-fact world of crime detection. Yet somehow, as Mr Tombe talked on, telling the detective of his own investigations, the dream seemed to take on a significance.

At length, Carlin leaned back in his chair. 'Very well, Mr Tombe,' he said. 'We'll look into the matter.' A day or two later, when Carlin and his men went down to The Welcomes, he discovered something that sent a shiver down his spine. *There were five disused wells in the grounds of the farm.*

Carlin remembered Mrs Tombe's dream. Perhaps a mother's intuition *had* probed beyond the veil. Ridiculous? Well, let's see. He gave the order – 'Dig.'

The autumn moon hung low over the stark, fire-blackened rafters of the gutted farmhouse. Somewhere away in the distance, a dog was howling. Otherwise, only the scraping of the spades on stones and the heavy breathing of the diggers broke the stillness.

Suddenly one of the men called out: 'We've come to water here, sir.' Then, as the glow of the lowered lantern tinctured the oily black surface twelve feet down, they saw, sticking out of the mud, a human foot.

Hours later, at Bandon Hill mortuary, near Wallington, Tombe's father looked at the body – at the stained clothes, the gold wrist-watch, the tie-pin, the cuff-links. Tears were running down his face as he whispered: 'Yes – yes. That is my dear boy.'

A pathologist discovered a gun-shot wound, about 1¼ inches in diameter, at the back of the head. He thought that it was probably caused by a shotgun, fired at close range.

What actually happened at The Welcomes must remain for ever a mystery. Not even the date of the murder is known. The coroner's jury put it as on or about 21 April 1922, but that was mere guesswork.

Carlin had his theories, though. He believed that Dyer had lured Tombe to The Welcomes and, in a tumble-down shed near the paddock, crept up from behind and shot him in the back of the head. He had left the body in the shed, returning later to stuff it down the well and fill the well with stones.

This theory was partly confirmed by a subsequent conversation with Dyer's widow. She told how, at about eleven o'clock one night, she was sitting alone at The Welcomes, when she heard the sound of stones dropping against the drainpipe. She called to her dog and opened the front-door. As she peered out, the dog started to growl and bristle. The moon was up, but big black clouds scudding across the sky plunged the yard into alternate silvery light and thick darkness. Suddenly, barking savagely, the dog dashed towards a disused shed in the corner of the yard and flew at someone crouching in the shadows. A man emerged, and at that moment a stream of moonlight flooded full on his face. To her astonishment, she saw that it was her husband, whom she had believed to be miles away, on business in France. Deathly pale and trembling, he held up his hands, shouting, 'Don't come in here. Don't come out. Get into the house again, for God's sake.'

Nearly seventy years have gone by since Tombe and Dyer perished – both by the same hand. But The Welcomes still stands.

When, some years ago, I went there, it was a peaceful scene. The wells had long since been filled in. Nothing remained to hint at the old tragedy.

Over a cup of tea in a luxuriously-furnished room above what were once the stables, the then occupant, the widow of Charles Pelly, the pilot who flew Neville Chamberlain to Munich on his 'Peace in Our Time' flight to see Hitler in 1938, told me: 'The Tombe tragedy wasn't the only one connected with The Welcomes, you know. In 1934 a Major St John Rowlandson shot himself in a taxi as he was being driven through St James's Street. I think he was in some sort of financial trouble. He lived here with his sister.'

But it was the Tombe case that was remembered in those parts. 'Even today,' said Mrs Pelly, 'local boys peer through the gate and recall "Eric down the well".'

What are the odds against anyone dreaming the same circumstantially accurate dream night after night, as the clergyman's wife did? If it was no more than chance, then they are odds so high that it is virtually impossible to calculate them.

And was it not passing strange that a hard-headed policeman should, acting on the 'evidence' of a mother's prophetic dream, come to solve what might well have remained a mystery for ever?

An Astrological Postscript

William Henry

Had Sherlock Holmes turned to the planets for help when unravelling some of his more celebrated murder-cases, we might today be surrounded by dozens of star-gazing 'astro-sleuths', each as eager to seek clues in a suspect's birth-chart as in the bloodstained clothing found under the floor-boards. But despite a life-long interest in the paranormal, Conan Doyle never let his pipe-smoking hero examine a single horoscope. And what a pity. For if he had, Sir Arthur might have forged some useful links between astrology and the law.

Holmes, of course, confined his detective work to the fiction shelf; but much can be said for the use of astrology in real-life murder investigations as well, for no matter how carefully a killer may try to cover his tracks, there is always one piece of evidence he can never destroy: namely, the positions of the planets at the time of his crime.

Which brings us to the Dyer-Tombe case. Did Ernest Dyer actually kill Eric Tombe? And if so, is there any evidence – any planetary evidence, I mean – to confirm that fact?

Before looking at what the planets have to tell us (and by tradition the Sun and Moon are called 'planets' as well), I should explain that in astrology one normally works with at least three sets of planetary positions: the 'natal' positions (those degrees of the zodiac occupied by the planets at the time of a person's birth); the 'progressed' positions (those degrees occupied by the planets during the days immediately following birth, where each day represents one year in the individual's life); and the 'transiting' positions (the actual day-to-day positions of the planets at any given time).

Since the planets act as the principal words in the language of astrology, every person, object or event encountered in life can be expressed by the appropriate

54

'signature' or combination of individual planets. Murder, for example, is commonly indicated by the 'vulgar' (Hades) 'acts' (Mars) combination of Mars and Hades (one of the eight transneptunian 'planets' discovered by Alfred Witte and his colleagues at the Hamburg School of Astrology), with Saturn or Uranus also frequently appearing as part of the signature.

To create a signature, the planets involved must be properly linked together. A link is formed, for example, whenever the distance between two planets is either an exact whole-number fraction of the full 360° zodiac or a whole-number multiple of that fraction, or whenever a planet is positioned either on the 'midpoint' (or halfway point) of two planets or at one of those same fractional distances from that midpoint. Thus, planets that are 45° apart (⅛ of 360°) or 135° apart (⅜ of 360°) will be linked together, as will any three planets, one of which is positioned either 30° (1/12), 60° (1/6), or 72° (1/5) away from the midpoint of the other two.

Now, if Ernest Dyer killed Eric Tombe (as the circumstantial evidence strongly suggests), then we ought to be able to find at least one Mars-Hades 'murder signature' in Dyer's chart at the time of Tombe's death. Ideally, such a signature should also be linked to Tombe's natal or progressed Sun − that is to say, to either the Sun's position when Tombe was born or (since Tombe was 29½ years old when he died) to its position 29½ days after he was born − in order to identify Tombe as the murder-victim.

Surprisingly enough, a link does turn up in Dyer's chart between Tombe's natal Sun (1° Scorpio) and Dyer's natal Hades (1° Pisces), for those two planets are exactly 120° (⅓ of the zodiac) apart. But Dyer's natal Mars (13° Leo), needed to complete the Mars-Hades 'murder' signature, is not directly connected to either of those planets.

The investigation, however, does not end there. If we calculate the position of Dyer's progressed Mars for the spring of 1922, note what turns up: at the time of Tombe's murder, Dyer's progressed Mars (1° Virgo) was exactly

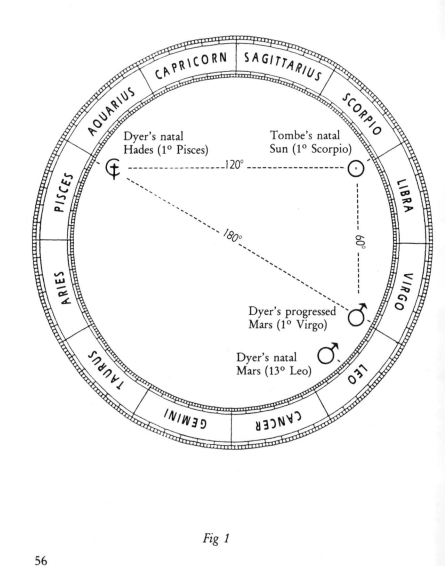

Fig 1

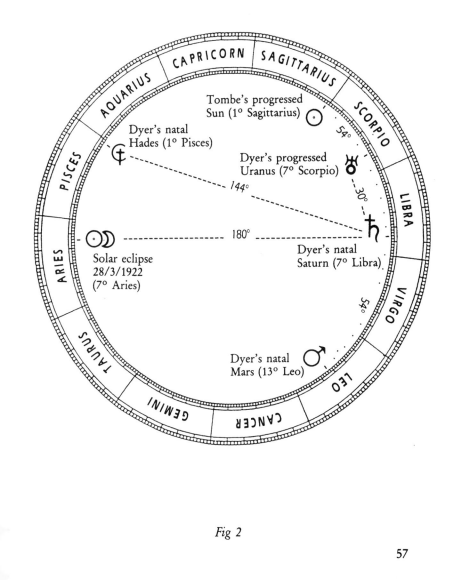

Fig 2

180° (½ of the zodiac) away from Dyer's natal Hades and 60° (⅙ of the zodiac) away from Tombe's natal Sun, thus creating the 'murder' signature linked to Tombe's Sun that we were looking for (Fig 1). To the astrologer, such evidence is as incriminating as the discovery of Tombe's suitcase in Dyer's possession in Scarborough.

But there is still more evidence to be found against Dyer. In his chart, natal Saturn (7° Libra) is linked to natal Hades (the distance between them is 144° or ⅖ of the zodiac) and at the time of Tombe's death was also linked to Dyer's progressed Uranus (30° away at 7° Scorpio). Had Dyer's natal or progressed Mars been part of this same pattern, we would once again have a potentially dangerous 'murder signature' on our hands − but Dyer's natal Saturn fails to reveal any obvious links to either of these Mars positions. However, if we measure the distance in his chart from natal Mars to natal Saturn, and similarly measure the distance from natal Saturn to the position of Tombe's progressed Sun (1° Sagittarius) in 1922, note what we discover: those two distances (54° each) are exactly the same − thus placing Dyer's natal Saturn (7° Libra) directly on the midpoint (7° Libra) formed between his natal Mars and Tombe's progressed Sun at the time of Tombe's death (Fig 2). In other words, *Tombe was killed precisely during that one brief period in his life when the position of his progressed Sun would complete the Mars-Saturn-Uranus-Hades 'murder pattern' in Dyer's horoscope.*

An ephemeris for 1922 (listing the daily positions of the planets) indicates that a solar eclipse took place in March of that year, less than a month before Tombe's death. The ancient astrologers feared eclipses, for they tend to act as powerful 'triggers' for any planets or planetary signatures to which they are attached. (For instance, the 15 January 1991 deadline set by the United Nations for the withdrawal of Iraqi troops from Kuwait fell on the day of a solar eclipse [at 25° Capricorn] that was directly linked to the position of Mars [the planet most commonly identified with weapons and warfare] in President Bush's natal horoscope.)

It therefore comes as no surprise to find that the March 1922 solar eclipse fell at 7° Aries, exactly opposite (that is to say, 180° away from) Dyer's natal Saturn, thus linking the eclipse-point to the entire cluster of planets (Mars, Uranus, Hades, and Tombe's progressed Sun) attached to Dyer's natal Saturn at that time!

If we knew the precise time of Dyer's (and of Tombe's) birth, we could possibly determine the exact day (and perhaps even the time of day) that Tombe was killed. In the absence of that evidence, we can note that Tombe was most likely murdered some time between 17 April (the date of his letter to his parents) and the 22nd (when he failed to keep his appointment). And we can further note that on Wednesday the 19th, the 'murder midpoint' between transiting Mars and transiting Hades was exactly aligned with the 'thinking about Tombe' midpoint formed by transiting Mercury in combination with Tombe's progressed Sun. This could easily have been a day on which Dyer thought seriously about killing Tombe, and may even have been the actual day that Dyer, eager to get his hands on Tombe's money, pointed a gun at Tombe's head and pulled the trigger. The exact time of the murder may never be known, but there can be little doubt (astrologically speaking) about the identity of Tombe's killer.

Calling Madame Isherwood . . .

EDMUND PEARSON

WHEN GHOSTS get into court, they meet a facetious and disrespectful audience. It used to be otherwise: there are some fine stories of spectral evidence in murder cases of two or three hundred years ago.

We laugh at the judge in the Salem witchcraft trials who rose and struck with a switch at the evil spirits that were floating in the air above the bench. But we listen with grave faces while the alienists in the Loeb-Leopold case [1924] talk about the 'king and slave phantasy'; or while a psychiatrist at the Hickman trial in California [1928] practises 'dermography' or skin-writing as a test of sanity.

The trouble with the clairvoyant, the dealer in ghosts, is that he is socially *déclassé*.

One of the spiritualists to come before an American court, and bring her ghosts with her, was an Englishwoman, a practising medium in New Bedford, Massachusetts. She called herself Madame Isherwood, and she was an important witness for the State in the trial of William Crockett Howard for the murder of his wife, Ida.

At that time, in 1908, Howard was a young fellow in his twenties; a native of Tennessee; and a private in the United States Army, stationed at Fort Rodman in New Bedford harbour. He was most unprepossessing, with a sullen face, and ugly, turned-down lips.

But he had the lure of his uniform, or else he had a way with him, for he devoted his spare time, most successfully, to love affairs. He made a list of his girls — it was found in his soldier's manual – during three years at the fort, setting down the Amys and Rosas and Fredas and Evas (there were three Evas) and Mollies and Adelines whose hearts he had won.

These were all in addition to his wife, whom he married in Tennessee during an interval between enlistments; and in addition to two other women – his real sweetheart, a girl far above him in character and in intellect, and still another, a pert little drab who came into court and committed perjury on his behalf.

It must be the soldier's facility in these conquests, with no more expenditure for entertainment than a few nickels for ice-cream cones and chewing gum, which turns so many literary men and artists into excited anti-militarists.

During Howard's courtship of Grace Sturtevant – the one superior woman he seems to have known – the two were in Hazelwood Park one evening, gazing at the moon, when there appeared a low fellow named Dewhurst, who said or did something highly objectionable.

I do not know what he did, but it was the final mistake in the life of Mr Dewhurst. He had insulted a lady, the United States Army, and one of the Fighting Howards of Tennessee. In a few seconds – for Private Howard proceeded to violence – the soul of Dewhurst had departed to its own place, while Howard and Miss Sturtevant were refugees from the park.

It was apparent, even to Howard, that the testimony of Miss Sturtevant, the only witness to the fight, was necessary to his safety. Moreover, he seems to have liked her, more or less, and she assuredly loved him, and expressed her devotion in a series of sincere and pathetic letters. Nevertheless, Howard, in the six weeks between his two enlistments, returned to Tennessee, where for some mysterious reason he married Ida Williams.

He was ordered back to Fort Rodman, and when he returned he brought Mrs Howard, whom he introduced as his sister, quartering her in the town.

He seems to have been annoyed with his wife from the

start. She, so he said, 'gave him away' to the police, so that he was arrested in the Dewhurst affair. Grace Sturtevant, although she now learned of his marriage, testified for him and secured his release by the court. He was held to have acted in self-defence. Next, Ida Howard had her husband arrested for non-support, and caused him to assign part of his pay to her. Finally, and as a crowning mark of her irritating disposition, she was going to have a baby.

Howard said that he wished to get rid of his wife − legally − and marry Miss Sturtevant. It is much more probable that he did not wish to marry anyone, but that he preferred to have a number of girls at his beck and call, ready to help him out of scrapes.

At all events, on a September night he told his sergeant that he was going to fish for eels; he took a boat and disappeared. His wife, the same evening, called on Madame Isherwood, the seeress, and told her that she had an appointment to meet her husband that night at a place on the bay, called Padanaram, where they were to look at a house they were to take for the winter. This place is three miles by water from the fort − easy rowing distance.

Next morning, Ida Howard's body was found there, floating in the water. Some of the doctors testified that she had not been drowned but had been strangled before being thrown overboard. Although a man and woman had been seen on the bridge, nobody had recognised either of the principals. Howard made eager attempts to get his fellow-soldiers to swear to an alibi. Altogether, it takes someone well practised in believing impossible things to put much trust in the soldier's innocence of murder.

Nevertheless, the testimony of Madame Isherwood, as establishing Ida Howard's intention to meet her husband that night, was essential to the case for the prosecution. The prisoner's counsel, Mr Morton (afterwards Judge Morton), made his best efforts to discredit the medium, and to ridicule her psychic faith. He afterwards gave Francis Wellman, the celebrated writer on cross-examination, an account of the questioning.

He asked the witness why she had delayed four weeks in telling about the call from Mrs Howard. She answered that she spoke only when the spirit of Ida Howard appeared to her and told her to reveal the story of the conversation. Mr Morton said that a wave of credulity seemed to sweep over the court; that the jury seemed influenced; and that, for a moment, he felt his case to be desperate. Then he saw his chance, and bombarded her with questions like these:

'What kind of a spirit was it? A plump spirit, above five feet high?' 'Did she have on spirit clothes?' 'Did this spirit carry a harp?' 'Or a halo?'

Finally, he asked: 'Did it appear to you frequently?'

The reply was 'Every night'.

Whereupon, with the delicate humour of the courtroom, the attorney inquired: 'Don't you take a glass of whisky every night before going to bed?'

Aside from the spiritualist, the women who surrounded Howard were of a wide variety, and the case was remarkable for their devotion. At one extreme was the girl who tried to establish an alibi for the soldier, by swearing that she was with him, in the reservation, on the evening of the murder. She was a tiny creature, named Lena Watson, but more intimately known as 'Bug' Watson. Her father was a portentous character of the water-front; the proprietor of a resort which it would be complimentary to call dubious. He was known as 'Devil Dan'.

His daughter wrote letters to Howard, signing herself 'Little Lena', but the District Attorney, displaying that frank realism which some of us praise in novelists but find so detestable when applied to a criminal or his friends, dismissed her as 'Little Liar'.

At the other extreme was Grace Sturtevant, a girl of eighteen or twenty, rather plain of feature, but well educated and with aspirations both to write and to paint pictures. While Howard was in Tennessee, getting married and re-enlisting in the Army, both contrary to his promises to her, she was writing to him:

My Sweetheart Will,

I have been so lonesome and sad tonight that I can only rest my mind by writing to you.... No truer heart ever beat for you than mine. I do love you with my whole heart.... Oh, Will, if you only knew how dearly I love you, you would not stay away from me so long.... This letter is written amidst tears. Do you realise how long you have been gone? Good night, love, and God bless you. That you may come back is my only prayer. From your true and trustworthy sweetheart,

GRACE

Whether it was the ridicule excited against Madame Isherwood or because of their own timidity in dealing with a pretty clear case, the jury debated a long time, and at last found Howard guilty of murder in the second [non-capital] degree. One of the jurors is said to have discovered – contrary to his oath – scruples against capital punishment.

When the prisoner was sentenced to a life term in the State Prison, his luck was still with him, and the law, like his sweethearts, was doing better by him than he deserved.

A Surfeit of Spirits

COMPILED BY JONATHAN GOODMAN

[COMPILER'S NOTE. I have put together this account of strange goings-on in Hammersmith (which is on the south-western edge of London, partly bounded by the U-shaped stretch of the Thames between Chiswick and Fulham) from criminal-court records at the Public Record Office and press clippings in a folder, marked GHOSTS: LOCAL, at the Hammersmith Public Library. Once or twice, I have altered tenses of press reports; I have put misspellings right, amended some of the punctuation, and whenever there were versions of the name of a person or place, chosen one of them. Chiefly because of the jigsaw nature of the compilation (I have sometimes inserted just a few words from one report in a paragraph from another), I have not cited individual sources; but the clippings I have used are from, among other papers, *Bell's Weekly Messenger*, the *Star*, the *Sunday Herald*, *The Times*, and the *West London Observer*. If anyone really needs to know which bits are from where, I am sure that Christine Bailey, at the Library, will be as helpful to him or her as she has been to me.]

> ... In the night, imagining some fear,
> How easy is a bush supposed a bear!
> *A Midsummer Night's Dream* (Act V, Scene 1)

Thursday, 5 January 1804 We have to announce to the public an event which in some of its circumstances is so ludicrous, but in its result so dreadful, that we fear that if the reader should laugh with one side of his mouth, he must of necessity cry with the other.

The neighbourhood of Hammersmith has of late been kept in a constant state of alarm, in consequence of the nocturnal appearance of what credulity supposed a Ghost. For many weeks past, the church-bell no sooner struck one than a spectre seemed to flit along the fields adjacent to Black Lion Lane, leading to the river. The old and young watched its coming, but preserved an awful distance. Women and children have nearly lost their senses. One poor woman, who was far advanced in her pregnancy of a second child, was so much shocked at this supposed Ghost that she took to her bed, where she still lies. The Ghost so much alarmed a waggoner belonging to Mr Russell, driving a team of eight horses, and with fifteen passengers at the time, that he took to his heels, leaving the waggon and horses so precipitately that the whole were greatly endangered. Neither man, woman nor child could pass that way for some time past; and the report was that it was the Apparition of a man who cut his throat in the neighbourhood above a year ago. Several lay in wait different nights for the Ghost; but there are so many by-lanes and paths leading to this riparian part of Hammersmith that he was always sure of being on that which was unguarded, and every night played his tricks to the terror of the populace.

So far back as October last, the first rumours of a Ghost were in circulation in the neighbourhood near the church. It was then reported that a mad woman was in the habit of disturbing the neighbours by perambulating the church-yard and other walks, in strange and uncouth dresses – which, after a little time, was discovered by Mr Moody, of the Six Bells, to be nothing more than a youth belonging to Mr Kilberton, a neighbouring butcher, who, by way of frolic and to plague the maid his fellow-servant, had dressed himself in her clothes, in which he frequently appeared in the church-yard and other places. Being reprimanded by Mr Moody and others, and warned of ill consequences which might attend his antics, he desisted from the practice altogether.

Notwithstanding, another Phantom soon sprang up, and was seen *all in white* at various places. This Ghost was so clever and nimble in its retreats that they never could be traced – till one evening when one Brazier, a chimney-sweep, going through the lower part of Church Lane, and the night being very dark, was alarmed at the appearance of this supposed Spectre; and as he related the story the next morning, it seems that he stood stock-still some moments before he durst proceed. However, having a stick in his hand, he extended it at arm's length; advancing towards the tree against which he saw the object, he was induced to exclaim: 'Ghost! or whatever you may be, pray be civil.' But as he still continued advancing with a slow pace, he, instead of penetrating a body of thin air, found his stick in contact with the clothes of a female, who proved to be a Miss G---, a young lady of Hammersmith, with her male companion.

After this discovery, nothing of the kind was seen or heard of in this quarter, excepting what has been related by Thomas Groom, a servant to Messrs Burgess and Winter, brewers. He, a stout and able man, asserted for a truth that he was nearly choked by the rude caresses of a Phantom which he met in the church-yard. He did not keep to his bed, as it is reported in some newspapers, but it was several days before he got the better of his fright.

The next disturber of the peace made its appearance not in the church-yard, but lower down, towards Beaver, Black Lion, and Plough & Harrow Lanes, which served it as a retreat when pursued from the high road. A drummer belonging to the Chiswick Volunteers, an inhabitant of Hammersmith, and a rat-catcher by his profession, was one of the first that was panic-struck by this Spectre. The next was a clerk to Mr Cromwell the brewer, who thought he saw a supernatural appearance about five o'clock one morning in Plough & Harrow Lane, and was considerably alarmed. The pretended Spectre, on Thursday, 29

December, made a more public appearance; for, as William Girdler, the watchman, came out of the house of Mrs Samuel, No 2 Queen's Place, adjoining Beaver Lane, an apprentice boy belonging to Mr James Graham the shoemaker ran across the road towards him, dreadfully frightened at what he supposed to be a Ghost! In consequence of this, the watchman looked towards the opposite side of the road, on the left hand of the pump, and was witness to an object all in white. Approaching the spot where it stood, he observed some person divest himself of a sheet or tablecloth, he could not distinguish which, wrap it up under his coat, and run away. Being dark, this person was soon out of sight. Girdler thereupon went to the White Hart, and inquired if any strange person was just come in there. While Girdler was going by, the pretended Ghost, it is supposed, hid behind Mr Hill's house; but leaving the spot in Girdler's absence, he was seen by some of Mr Hill's family, who observed a corner of the white cloth hanging below his coat. While he stood near the pump, he was also seen by a Mrs Steward, and her servant, at No 4 Theresa Terrace, who were both much alarmed.

We come now to the afflicting part of the relation, describing how the Christmas tricks of the Goblin have terminated in a melancholy incident.

On Tuesday last, a young Officer of Excise named Francis Smith, who is stated to be twenty-nine years of age, having spent part of his evening at the White Hart, left it, perfectly sober, with the purpose of passing the remainder at a private party to which he had been invited; but by some means or other his purpose was changed, and he returned to the White Hart, where a conversation about the Ghost took place; Mr Smith thereupon went next door to his lodgings, at the house of Mr Oakley, to collect his fowling-piece, which he brought back to the White Hart, loaded it there with powder and shot, and said he would act this night, go and try to meet the Ghost, and certainly shoot it. It was just past eleven o'clock. Mr Smith preconcerted with the watchman, William Girdler, to go up one lane while he, Mr Smith, went round by another, the reputed haunt of the Ghost; the two men agreed upon a pass-word, whereby they might distinguish each other, which was — 'Who comes there?' 'A friend.' 'Advance, friend.' They sallied out.

As Mr Smith came through Cross Lane, at the end of Black Lion Lane, he saw a man dressed in white, whom he challenged, and asked who he was. The person made no answer. The night was very dark. After a minute or two, he challenged him again, and told the person in white that if he did not answer, he would certainly shoot him. The man made no answer, and Mr Smith levelled his piece and shot him through the head.

The poor man expired on the spot, the ball having entered his mouth and gone out at the back part of his skull. He was subsequently conveyed to the Black Lion, and there recognised as Thomas Milward, who was by trade a plasterer and bricklayer.

Mr Smith readily surrendered himself to Mr John Lock, a wine merchant in Hammersmith, who was returning home from the Plough & Harrow. Mr Smith told Mr Lock that he had been in great trepidation when the Ghost, instead of answering when he was called upon, had advanced straight towards him. Mr Lock has said that the event took place between two high hedges, so that it was really difficult to discover the body.

Meanwhile, William Girdler had heard the gun fired; but he did not take any notice of it, as he had often heard guns firing in the night-time. He himself was armed with a pistol, as was his usual custom. Eventually coming upon Messrs Lock and Smith, he learned of what had transpired, and accompanied them to the White Hart.

At six o'clock yesterday [Wednesday] evening, Mr Smith was brought in custody of the Bow Street officers from the White Hart, where he had been since the incident, to town, and was committed to Newgate Prison.

Both parties lived in, and were well known to, the neighbourhood. The deceased, who was twenty-three years

of age, was in his working dress, which consisted of white
linen trousers and a white waistcoat, the trousers being
very long, almost touching the shoes. Ann Milward, the
sister of the deceased, said that she lived with her parents,
and that betwixt the hours of ten and eleven on the fateful
night, her brother (who lived at his father-in-law's) came to
the house and said he had been seeking for his wife, who
was at a Mr *Smith's*; the sister, as well as her father and
mother, were just going to bed. She asked her brother to
sit down, which he did, remaining about half an hour; he
then bade his parents and his sister good-night and walked
out, having heard the watchman calling the hour. The
sister, being almost immediately struck with a presenti-
ment that some accident would befall him, accordingly
went to the door and stood on some bricks in order to look
out for him. She then heard a voice say, 'D--n you, who are
you? Stand, else I'll shoot you!' and the report of a gun
immediately succeeded. She called out, '*Thomas!*' and
returned to her mother, saying to her, 'I believe my brother
is shot.' Neither her father nor her mother would believe
it. She then went out, and discovered her brother lying
perfectly dead. She returned home very much shocked. She
had often heard of the Ghost, and it was described in
various ways, but was said to be dressed particularly in
white, with long horns and glass eyes; she had never
thought of cautioning her brother of any danger he might
be in from wearing a dress so similar in appearance to that
of the Ghost. She knows nothing of any animosity sub-
sisting betwixt the deceased and Mr Smith; and she believes
they hardly knew each other but by sight.

Monday, 9 January 1804 To the satisfaction of most of
the inhabitants of the town and neighbourhood of
Hammersmith, the *real* Ghost has at last been discovered
in the person of one James Graham.

The much lamented sacrifice of poor Milward had such
a powerful effect that last Thursday evening an information
was lodged before Mr Hill, the Magistrate, against a

housekeeper in the town of Hammersmith, a boot and shoe-maker, who has a wife and three children, for going out at night wrapped up in a blanket, with a design to represent a Ghost! He was consequently taken into custody and examined before the said Magistrate, who, doubtful how to act without advice in such a case, took bail for his appearance. The people of Hammersmith expected that the Ghost was yesterday to have stood publicly in the Church, wrapped up in a white sheet, by way of penance, and vast numbers were consequently collected to behold such a spectacle!

Graham, when questioned by the Magistrate as to the cause of his assuming such a disguise, said that he had done it in order to be revenged on the impertinence of his apprentices, who had terrified his children – and, to a lesser degree, his lodger, the one-armed postman – by telling them stories of Ghosts. He expected to check them of this disagreeable bent of their mind to the prejudice of his children by presenting them, as they passed homewards, with a figure of a ghost – which, it seems, he managed very successfully. Had this weak, perhaps wicked, frolic ended here, it is likely that no serious consequences would have ensued.

This Graham, it is to be noticed, is a constant attendant, and one of the first singers, at Trinity Church, and always bore an excellent character till now. He might think that his singing at the funeral of poor Milward would be some reparation for the folly in which he has been so deeply implicated.

It would engross too much of the reader's attention to state minutely the disagreeable results of his different experiments. The report that a lady of Brooke Green, far advanced in pregnancy, had died in consequence of the appearance of the Spectre, we are happy to find is totally unfounded; she, having received her fright from a person in a state of intoxication, soon recovered from a mere feeling of faintness.

The various reports going around Hammersmith would

more than fill a newspaper – some absolutely affirming that they had seen the eyes of the ghost appear like a *glow worm* – others that he *breathed fire and smoke* – and others again that he vanished in a moment, and sunk in the earth in their presence! Notwithstanding the discovery and detection, very few will yet venture out after dark, so dreadful has been the impression made on the minds of the inhabitants by Graham, who has been obliged to answer for these wanton and manifold outrages of the public peace by the payment of a fine that by many is considered a paltry price to pay.

Old Bailey, Friday, 13 January 1804 Francis Smith was indicted for the wilful murder of Thomas Milward, in Hammersmith, on 3 January instant.

The prisoner was dressed in black, and conducted himself throughout the trial with decent firmness. During the time he remained at the bar, his countenance did not appear to express much agitation, until the jury left the box.

Counsel for the Crown called four witnesses: Mr John Lock, wine merchant in Hammersmith; William Girdler, a watchman; Ann Milward, a very genteel young woman, sister of the deceased; and Mr Flower, a surgeon, who deposed that he examined the body of the deceased and found that he had received a gun-shot wound in the lower part of the left jaw; it appeared to have been occasioned by a ball of the size of No 4; it had penetrated the vertebra of the neck and had injured the spinal marrow of the brain. He entertained no doubt of the wound having been the real and sole cause of the deceased's death; it disfigured the jaw, and he observed that the face was all blackened with the powder from the gun, indicating that it had been fired at close range.

The prisoner, on being called on for his defence, said he would leave it to his counsel; but, on being told by the Judge, the Lord Chief Baron, that counsel could not speak in his behalf, he stated that on the day on which that fatal catastrophe happened, he went out with a good intention, and at the very moment of the affair taking place he did not know what he was doing. He spoke to the person twice, and was so much agitated on receiving no answer that, in his confusion and dread, he was unfortunate enough to commit the rash action; but he solemnly declared to God that he had no malice against the deceased, nor any intention of taking away the life of any individual whatever.

His counsel then proceeded to call the witnesses on his behalf.

The first was Mrs Phebe Foulbrook, mother-in-law of the deceased. She stated that she had frequently heard of the Ghost. On the Saturday evening preceding her son-in-law's death, he had said to her that he had been taken for the Ghost on account of the dress he wore, and that two ladies and a gentleman had been frightened at him on the Terrace. One of them cried as he came near, 'Here comes the Ghost!' To which he replied, using a bad oath, 'I am no more a Ghost than yourself; do you want a punch o' the head?' On hearing this, the witness had advised him to put on a great-coat for fear of accidents, and not to frighten any person again.

A great many other witnesses were then called, one to speak of the supposed Ghost, and the others to speak solely to the prisoner's character; all of the latter concurred in giving him one of the very best, and proved that he was a young man of a remarkably mild temper, and of a humane, generous and benevolent disposition.

The Lord Chief Baron then charged the jury. It would, he observed, be necessary for him to state that although, to constitute the crime of murder, it was generally requisite that *malice propense* should be proved, yet it was not absolutely so in all cases. The law did not of necessity imply that where a person met his death from the hands of another, malice, or what was called spite in vulgar speaking, should be proved. The disposition of a person's mind to kill was sufficient, in the eye of the law, to adjudge him guilty of murder. For instance, if some person should have taken

73

it into his head to fire into the very hall in which the Court was sitting, and kill anyone in the Court, then he would be guilty of murder. So, in another case, if a person should shoot at one man and kill another, he would be equally guilty. The law would consider his disposition of mind, which was evidently to kill, without having legal authority or just provocation, not in self-defence, nor in the absence of his reasoning faculty. His Lordship professed that he could not, in this case, distinguish any one of these features of alleviation or mitigation; therefore, if the prisoner at the bar had taken away the life of another, his offence was murder. If that was not so, no one could be safe; it would be in the power of anyone to say, such and such a one has committed some offence which I think deserves death, and I will go and despatch him. It was fortunate that the law of this country has deemed such an offence to be murder. In the present case, it was sufficient to endeavour to apprehend; but not to kill. If, therefore, the jury entertained no doubt with respect to the fact, he would betray his duty, and injure the public security, if he did not persist in asserting that this was a clear case of murder, if the facts were proved to the jury's satisfaction. In cases of some involuntary acts, or some sufficiently violent provocation, killing became manslaughter. Not one of those circumstances occurred here. There was here no apparent intention of the prisoner to apprehend this person; instead of that, which would have been the proper step in such a case, he was proved to have taken out a gun in order to shoot him, erroneously imagining he was entitled to do so. If the jury believed the facts presented, they would find the prisoner guilty. His Lordship observed that the character which had been given of the prisoner was of no avail here.

The jury retired for an hour and a quarter, and on their return delivered a verdict of Guilty of Manslaughter.

The Lord Chief Baron informed them that the Court could not receive such a verdict; they were bound by the solemn obligation which they had taken, to decide according to the facts. If they believed the evidence, their verdict must be Guilty; if they discredited the witnesses, they would acquit the prisoner. It was not for them to assume the King's prerogative and mitigate the punishment.

The jury were desired to reconsider and amend their verdict, which they accordingly did forthwith, without leaving the box. The verdict was Guilty.

The Recorder then pronounced the awful sentence of death upon the prisoner, who seemed to be very much affected by his unfortunate situation. Silence being called, the Recorder addressed him nearly as follows:

'Francis Smith, you have been tried by a most attentive and intelligent jury, to whom the law on this unhappy case has been fully and ably stated. It was incumbent on you to have given evidence in mitigation of your heinous offence, if any such proof could possibly have been adduced. That not having been done, the jury have very properly, and according to law, found you guilty of the wilful murder of Thomas Milward. The law of God and man is that whosoever sheddeth man's blood shall atone for his offence by his own.' The prisoner was then sentenced, in the usual manner, to be executed on Monday next.

He was so much agitated that he was unable to walk from the dock without the assistance of two of the keepers. Mr Dignum, of Drury Lane Theatre, who had sat near him throughout the proceedings, was extremely affected; he wept, clasped his hands together, and suffered the greatest agitation. Several of the prisoner's relatives were also present, and apparently in great distress.

The Sessions House was still crowded in every part at nine o'clock, and the Yard was filled with an anxious multitude, all making inquiry, and interested in the fate of the prisoner. He was, as usual, taken back to Newgate; but at seven in the evening a respite arrived for him, till His Majesty's pleasure should be known.

Friday, 20 January 1804 The sentence of death passed upon

75

Francis Smith has been commuted to imprisonment for one year.

Tuesday, 20 January 1807 At the Kensington petty sessions yesterday, a bald-pated, grey-headed old man, named James Graham, the individual who caused such excitement in the neighbourhood of Hammersmith some years since by enacting the part of a Ghost, and during the pursuit of whom a man was unfortunately shot, was charged, with another man, named Joseph Mitchell, before Mr Codd, the sitting magistrate, with having been drunk and disorderly on Saturday night at Hammersmith.

Police Constable Dowling stated that, between twelve and one o'clock on Saturday night, while he was conveying a disorderly prostitute to the station-house, the prisoners interfered and created such a disturbance that he and other officers were obliged to take them into custody. They were first requested to go home quietly, but they declared they would go where they ---- pleased, and cursed and swore very much. They had both evidently been partaking of drink. Inspector Mullins and Policeman Ayres, T167, corroborated the evidence of Dowling.

His Ghostship, in his defence, addressed the bench in a whining voice, as follows:

'Sirs, on Saturday evening I went to the pawnbroker's to fetch home my best coat, for I always go two or three times on the Lord's day to a place of worship, and I like to go respectable. You have heard that I am charged with swearing. Now, as I am a worshipper of the true God, the great Jehovah, is it probable I would do so? I am a quiet spirit; and I associate, to quote the language of David, with "the excellent of the earth, in whom is my delight".

'I am not a frequenter of low public-houses, Sirs, but went into the Hammersmith coffee-house, and had half-a-pint of warm ale. While there, my companion came in and asked me to have a glass of ale; I said, "Thank ye, but yours is fourpenny, and mine sixpenny." We, however, had three pints of ale together, and when we came out the streets were in a very quiet state. Sirs, there is usually more than a hundred persons in the streets of Hammersmith at that time on a Saturday night, but then they were very quiet, more so than I have seen for years. I suppose it was owing to the working people having so little work, and consequently little money to spend.

'Well, Sirs, as we were going home, we met a tender female between two policemen, who were conducting her to the station-house. I said to my companion, "What a dreadful pity that a delicate woman should be locked up on such a cold night." The policeman said that if I interfered he would lock me up too. I immediately exclaimed, "Lock me up! Impossible! I never violated the laws of my country. I never injured man nor mortal." I then went to the station-house.

'Now, Sirs, could it be possible that I could be drunk? I'm a man who never will take spirits, and therefore was not drunk; I was just going home to my poor old woman, and to a warm bed, but they put me instead into what they call a cell, with boards for bed, and a block of wood for my pillow, by which I yesterday was prevented from enjoying what has been a blessing to me, the worship of my great Creator, the great God. I am not an ignorant man, Sirs, I can give you a description of the great God in language of —'

Mr Codd: 'Stop! I cannot take my ideas of God from the description of a man who frequents public-houses until twelve o'clock on Saturday nights.'

His Ghostship was fined five shillings, and Mitchell one shilling, or fourteen days in the House of Correction.

In 1825, Hammersmith was again the haunt of 'a Ghost whose mischievous antics spread dismay among young and old by nightly prancing about the vicinity, annoying every individual that chanced to fall within his perambulations' — till, at one o'clock one morning, Nicholas Worsley, returning home from Kensington, and having got as far as Widow Salter's turnpike-gate in Walham Green, encountered 'a man on horse-back, clothed in a white sheet, and with a hairy cap tied under his chin, who was making a most hideous groaning noise; rather than retreating, Worsley went forward and seized the bridle-rein of the Ghost's horse, took the white sheet off and threw it into a gentleman's garden, forced the Ghost to dismount, and held on to him until a watchman, Isaac Hawkins, came up'. The offender turned out to be John Benjamin, 'a quite respectable looking young farmer and hay-salesman of Alperton, in the parish of Harrow [seven or eight north-western miles by road from Walham Green]'. Next morning, up before a magistrate, he had no more to say in his defence than that he had been 'put in a joking mood' by a few too many drinks at a White Hart public-house other than the one associated with the shooting of Thomas Milward. 'The magistrate considered his behaviour a joke of too serious a nature to be lightly passed over, and ordered his Ghostship to find bail, himself of £50, and two sureties of £25 each, for his appearance at the Middlesex Sessions.' A few days later, a jury there found him guilty of unlawfully disguising himself with an intent to frighten His Majesty's subjects, and he was fined £10, with a warning that 'further sillinesses' would be punished more severely.

One hundred and thirty years later, in 1955, someone in Hammersmith remembered (or, as likely, invented) a supernatural tradition — that, every fifty years, on the August night when the moon was full, the ghost of a man who had cut his throat near St Paul's Church in 1803 appeared in the churchyard: 'therefore', going by the lunar data in *Old Moore's Almanack*, he could be expected on Wednesday, 3 August. Never minding the apparent quirkiness of the arithmetic — for if the ghost's stroll was an every-half-century anniversary one, he should have taken it in 1953 — journalists made up pieces about what might be going to happen. Interviews were published:

A resident of Hammersmith for over 70 years, who declined to give his name, said that he saw the ghost 50 years ago, 'wearing a white winding sheet, its eyes flaming'. Generations of his family, right back to his great-grandmother, have seen it. His great-grandmother was one of the first to see it when it began to appear between December 1803 and January 1804. She had been walking through the churchyard when 'a tall white figure rose from the tombs' and chased her until she fainted. When she recovered, the ghost had disappeared. Two days later she died.

Another elderly native of Hammersmith said that he had already had four 'ghostly experiences':

His first was in an empty house at Batoum Gardens [Hammersmith], where a murder is said to have been committed. He was going up the stairs in the dark when something brushed by him. 'It couldn't have been anything else but a ghost,' he says. During the battle of Mons in the First World War, he saw the famous 'Mons Angel' just before he was wounded. Before his demob, he was billeted in Lord Onslow's mansion in Ireland. One night he was on the ground floor when the housekeeper's dog came running down the stairs 'with the hair on its back stiff'. He then heard screams from the housekeeper and shouts of 'I've seen a ghost'. Then she fell down the stairs. He also claims to have seen the famous [sic] Hurlingham polo-ground ghost.

What with all the advance publicity, the churchyard was crowded on the Wednesday night. A detachment of policemen tried to keep order, and, sometimes failing, removed 'disorderly elements' (teddy boys, most of them) to a Black Maria parked outside the gate. According to one of the attending reporters, seventeen spectators (among them, the man who had had four 'ghostly experiences') were convinced that they had seen the anniversarial ghost − in the form of a flickering glow on the west wall of the church. No one bothered to count the people who, having seen the self-same glow, assumed it to be the remnant of a street-light, shining through breeze-blown foliage.

Reverting to the murder of Thomas Milward: though 'Smith' is a common name, it is a trifle odd that two Smiths were involved in the Hammersmith case – Francis, the murderer, and the Smith who, because Milward's wife was with him, was partly responsible for Milward's being out late at night looking for her. The latter Smith receives only a brief, unforenamed mention in a couple of the first press reports. (The name is italicised in the one I have used: I have no idea why.)

Other things seem odd:

When Francis Smith left the White Hart the first time, he was supposed to be going to a 'private party to which he had been invited'. It was then about half-past ten – an extraordinarily late time to be turning up at a party on a week-night.

'By some means or other his purpose was changed, and he returned to the White Hart, where a conversation about the Ghost took place....' What *were* the means that changed his purpose? Did he, returning, join in a conversation about the Ghost – or did he start it?

Odder than all the rest of the oddities is the fact (at last we have one) that when Francis Smith fired his gun, he was so close to Milward – or, presumably as he thought, a ghost – that the victim's face 'was all blackened with the powder'. Yes, it was a dark night – but, in the absence of evidence that Smith's vision was defective (and remembering that he had been out for at least a few minutes, long enough for his eyes to have grown accustomed to the darkness – so accustomed that he could see that Milward's waistcoat and trousers were white), it is hard to understand how he mistook a man for a ghost. Perhaps fear – and a certain tipsiness (for the report that he was 'perfectly sober' takes some swallowing) – caused a finger-jerk reaction.

Put together, the above oddities and unanswered

questions come nowhere near making a basis for a suspicion that the murder *of Milward* was premeditated.

However, a writer of fiction could easily transform the case into a tale:

The two Smiths are actually one and the same — a young Excise Officer who is carrying on an illicit affair with Milward's wife. She, having been told by Milward that he has been hired for a through-the-night job on commercial premises, arranges a tryst with Francis Smith at his lodgings at 10.30pm. As soon as Milward leaves, she dolls herself up — but he returns, asks her to explain her undomestic attire, and thus starts a row. Either he, already suspicious of her infidelity, has lied to her that he will be away all night — or she, in the course of the row, keen to cap a rude remark of his, screams that he is being cuckolded by a man named Smith. Then she flounces out. Milward goes in search of her. At 10.30, Francis leaves the White Hart for the 'private party' at his lodgings next-door, finds Mrs Milward in a state, and believes her exaggeration that Milward is searching for them both, meaning to commit double-murder. He, recalling that Milward has been mistaken for the ghost, has what seems to him to be a bright idea. Without thinking once, let alone twice, he hurries back to the pub, starts a conversation about the ghost, feigns a rush of blood to the head, collects his gun, and persuades Girdler the watchman to go one way — increasingly distant from where Milward is probably prowling — while he goes in that other direction. He finishes up at the house where Milward's parents and sister live; seeing Milward through the window, he waits, almost opposite the house, hiding in a gap between the high hedges. Milward comes out. Francis blocks his path, at the same time dashing off the words: 'Damn you, who are you? Stand, else I'll shoot you!' Not giving the perplexed Milward (*his* eyes certainly unaccustomed to the dark) time to answer, Francis kills him.

His cover-story seems perfect. *Seems*: he has not taken account of the legal definition of murder. Even so (and especially so at the time of this tale, in the early 1800s, when more than 210 offences less serious than murder can be punished by execution), a sentence of twelve months' imprisonment is a most inadequate penalty.

There can, if the fiction-writer wants a happy ending, be one: The Widow Milward, sticking to the promise she made stealthily before the trial, is waiting discreetly for Francis when he, having been a well-behaved convict, is let out early from prison, and they live contentedly in sin (always a long way from Hammersmith) ever after.

Amityville Revisited

JEFFREY BLOOMFIELD

OURS IS A WORLD of symbols, fast-flashing to awaken slumbering memories or ideas, much as Pavlov's bells awoke the salivary glands of his dogs. Addresses are such symbols. Is not the image of power or government awoken by the terms '1600 Pennsylvania Avenue', '10 Downing Street', 'the Kremlin'? What historical images are conjured up by the words 'Nineveh', 'the Great Wall', 'the Pyramids'? Words can also revive less pleasant memories: talk to a survivor of Nazi atrocities, and just see what a word like 'Dachau' can do. Lesser nightmares are there as well: the address '10 Rillington Place' will always evoke that tall, bald, seedy man in his horrible kitchen. The subject of this essay is also tied to an address: 112 Ocean Avenue, Amityville, New York. But though mass-murder occurred there, its infamy was made afterwards ... possibly with some paranormal help.

One Man's Family

To the east of Manhattan, the heart of New York City, is a long (120-odd mile) island, known, quite expectedly, as 'Long Island'. It is made up of four state-counties: Kings, Queens, Nassau, and Suffolk. The western two are among the five boroughs that make up the city of Greater New York (to add to this split-personality in geography, Kings County is actually the 'city' of Brooklyn, which, if independent, would be the fourth largest city in the United

States). Nassau County comes after Kings and Queens, but
the largest of the four counties is Suffolk, which stretches
into the Atlantic like the tail-end of a fish. Close to the foot
of the Nassau-Suffolk border is the small town of
Amityville. Its portion of Suffolk County faces down to
South Oyster Bay, which would lead directly into the
Atlantic Ocean, were it not for a strip of land comprising
Jones Beach and Gilgo State Park.

In 1974, Amityville had a population of about 10,000.
Like most communities on Long Island, the majority of the
working inhabitants had jobs in New York City; most of
the residents were in the upper middle class. A typical
resident was Mr Ronald DeFeo, who in 1974 was forty-
three years old. He had lived in Amityville since 1965,
when he had purchased the house at 112 Ocean Avenue. It
was a three-storey colonial-style house, and he had added
what he considered improvements to it, including a
swimming pool. It also had a two-car garage; also a boat-
house and pier, so that the family could take their boat out
into the bay. The newspapers of 1974 estimated the value
of the house as between $75,000 and $100,000. My knowledge of real-estate values is not the best, but I imagine that,
with inflation, the house has to be worth over $450,000 on
today's market. Given his investment, Ronald DeFeo had
a good feeling about his property, and even put up a sign
on his lawn saying 'High Hopes'.

In November 1974, the household comprised seven
people. Besides the father, there were Louise, his wife
(forty-two), Ronnie Jr (twenty-three), Dawn (eighteen),
Allison (thirteen), Mark (twelve), and John Matthew
(seven). Reporters for the New York papers questioned
neighbours about the family, and (with one glaring exception) learned nothing that was not nice or praiseworthy
about them. It was a close family, which 'prayed together,
travelled together, and threw snowballs together',
according to an article by George Vecsey in the *New York
Times* of Friday, 15 November. It was also considered a
charitable family, having befriended an elderly woman

84

named Catherine O'Reilly, whose husband had recently died. It was a conspicuously religious family: Ronald DeFeo had erected a creche on his front lawn that depicted St Joseph holding the Christ child, with three women kneeling to their saviour.

Ronald DeFeo worked as service manager at the Brigante-Karl Buick automobile dealership on Coney Island Avenue, Brooklyn. This firm was owned by DeFeo's father-in-law, Michael Brigante, and John Ventieri. The *New York Post* (14 November 1974) quoted the used-car sales manager, James Manitta, as saying that DeFeo was 'a happy-go-lucky guy who was well-liked by everybody. He didn't have an enemy in the world.' Again, the image of a nice person comes out, to be recalled later.

The exception to the 'lovely-family' stories was Ronnie Jr. Harry Stathos, writing in the *New York Daily News* (15 November), described him as a spoiled brat. It is hard to dispute the image. His parents showered him with gifts, like new cars, a $5000 boat, his own pool-room, and a stereo system. They were not totally tolerant, however: when he had a party once, his mother and he had a screaming match because he was playing the stereo too loud; it seems that the rest of the family wanted to sleep.

Ronnie did not have many school-friends. His personality turned them off, and his attempts to impress them by flashing large wads of dollars did not help. Neither did the two boys he hired as bodyguards, nor his stories about how his father had connections with the Mob.[1] Finally, he gave up on school and 'dropped out'. However, he got a high-school-equivalency diploma, and started working for the automobile agency as a mechanic in 1972. He retained his character-flaws. To avoid quarrels with him, his co-workers always said 'please' whenever they asked him to do anything.

---

1. As a result of Ronnie Jr's bragging and lies, an unfair rumour exists to this day that Ronald DeFeo had Mob connections. When the newspapers first covered the crime, they linked Ronald to one Peter DeFeo, a member of the Genovese Crime Family, saying Peter was his father. Ronald's father was Joseph DeFeo, who was not a gangster.

On Tuesday, 12 November 1974, Ronald and Ronnie Jr went to work. They seemed amicable enough. The next day, only Ronnie appeared. This did not concern anybody, as the older DeFeo was often away on business. That same Wednesday morning, a neighbour noticed the DeFeos' station-wagon in the driveway at the time when it was normally used to drive the younger children to school. Being a good neighbour, she minded her own business.

Ronnie left work between noon and one in the afternoon. He was not seen again for several hours. At four, a man named John Ballo was at Henry's Bar, half a mile from the DeFeo house, when he saw Ronnie driving past. Ballo invited him in. Ronnie looked dejected; he explained that he had had an argument with his parents and they had thrown him out of the house. He asked Ballo for a loan of $20. Ballo agreed, but said that he had to make a phone-call first. When he returned, Ronnie was gone. But he was reported as returning three times, once (according to the bartender) at five, having his favourite drink, a vodka and 7-Up.

Ronnie claimed later that he went home, found the house locked, and had to climb through a window to enter. Between 6.15pm and 6.30pm he *may* have called the police. At about 6.40pm, he returned to the bar, yelling as he entered: 'My father and mother have been shot.' Half a dozen men ran from the bar to the DeFeo house, saw dead bodies, and telephoned the emergency number, 911. The Suffolk County Police arrived at 7pm. All of Ronnie Jr's family were found shot in their respective bedrooms.

From the start, there were serious cracks in the crime. A neighbour made the astute Sherlockian observation: 'I don't see how anybody could have gotten in that house with the DeFeos' dogs around.' Despite the noise that so much shooting must have made, few people had heard anything unusual. Five neighbours recalled hearing the barks of Shaggy, the DeFeos' sheepdog, on Tuesday night; they had not considered that unusual, for Shaggy had a reputation as a barker in the off-hours. Patrick Mellon, the

Chief of Detectives for Suffolk County, failed to find traces of any struggle or break-in. A preliminary report from the coroner, at 10pm, estimated that the family had been dead about twenty-four hours. All of the bodies were in sleeping attire, face-down on their beds. Both parents had been shot twice in the head, and the siblings once each in the back. As there was no sign of the murder-weapon, a force of fifty Suffolk County detectives, and a dozen village policemen, started a search of the area, including using a metal-detector in the muddy Amityville Creek at the back of the house. Naturally, Ronnie Jr was closely questioned. As the sole surviving member of the family, he was taken into police custody, ostensibly 'for his protection'. When Mellon was asked if there were any suspects, he carefully replied: 'No one has been eliminated.'

It is obvious that the police were convinced of Ronnie's guilt from the start, but held their tongues while evidence was gathered against him. Within a few days, they located a .35-calibre Marlin rifle in the creek; the full coroner's report, released on 18 November, stated that it was the murder-weapon. The investigators reasoned that the victims had been drugged at dinner by Ronnie, probably with a barbiturate, so that they would be asleep while he killed them. According to the police, Ronnie voluntarily confessed that he had killed his brother Mark – but none of the others. Ronnie would insist that the confession was beaten out of him; the attorney representing him at this time mentioned that his body showed bruises caused during questioning. This would become a cornerstone of his defence.

Many unpleasant facts about Ronnie came out in the first few days ... facts that were to be almost submerged under wild surmises by interested parties within three years. He had a police record. In September 1973, he and a friend had stolen an outboard motor; in December, the charge of grand larceny was reduced to petty larceny; Ronnie got one year on probation. In April 1974, after his girlfriend had told the police that he was using drugs, a probation officer had found track-marks on his arm, and subsequent analysis revealed traces of quinine (used to dilute heroin) in his urine. In May 1974, a judge authorised probation officers to check him for drugs: of fifteen urine analyses carried out between May and October, two revealed the presence of quinine. In November 1974, Ronnie and a fellow-worker were given cheques and cash totalling $19,000 to deposit for the automobile dealership. They reported that, while they were still in the auto showroom, they were robbed of the money by a man with a gun. Ronnie must have sounded unconvincing, for, according to the *New York Times* (17 November), his father was visibly worried by his replies to police questions, and asked the police to be gentle with him.[1]

It adds to the poignancy and tragedy of this case that the DeFeos went out of their way to protect Ronnie Jr. When the drug-traces were found, they refused to accept the findings. With more serious charges, the father tried to get the police to 'go easy'. Notice how the theft of the outboard-motor became a petty larceny charge in December 1973: no doubt the older DeFeo talked to the authorities there too. It is just possible that the parents saw, at last, that they had to face reality. Ronnie's comment to John Ballo, that he had been thrown out of the house, may have referred to the outcome of a confrontation about the stolen money. After all, the $19,000 came from the family business: stealing it was like biting the protective hand.

The sole weakness in the prosecution's homicide case was that no central motive was ever found. The prosecution suggested that Ronnie was seeking a strongbox containing money in the house. I suspect that the $19,000 theft was the final item in a long, long list of sins that broke the family-ties. Perhaps he promised to repay the stolen cash so as to save himself from being thrown out or handed over to the police, and then used the temporary respite to make his

1. Charges relating to the theft of the $19,000 were brought against Ronnie Jr and his co-worker, Arthur Belin, on 15 November 1974. By that time, the former had other matters calling for his complete attention.

88

A Surfeit of Spirits

'Shooting a Ghost': a drawing by Phiz (Hablot Knight Browne)

Amityville Revisited

The house on Ocean Avenue: a recent photograph by Jan Zyniewski

Defending the 'Witch-Burners'

T.H. Matteson's painting The Trial of George Jacobs *(1855). The witnesses against Jacobs included one of his grand-daughters; after he had been hanged, she confessed that she had testified only because other witnesses had blackmailed her.*

Detail of Matteson's Examination of a Witch *(1853): a suspect is searched for 'witches' marks'.*

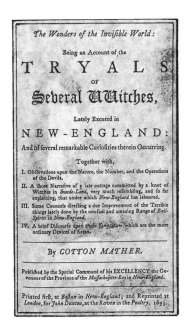

The Wonders of the Invisible World:

Being an Account of the

T R Y A L S

OF

Several Witches,

Lately Excuted in

N E W - E N G L A N D :

And of several remarkable Curiosities therein Occurring.

Together with,

I. Obfervations upon the Nature, the Number, and the Operations of the Devils.

II. A fhort Narrative of a late outrage committed by a knot of Witches in *Swede-Land*, very much refembling, and fo far explaining, that under which *New-England* has laboured.

III. Some Councels directing a due Improvement of the Terrible things lately done by the unufual and amazing Range of *Evil-Spirits* in *New-England*.

IV. A brief Difcourfe upon thofe *Temptations* which are the more ordinary Devices of Satan.

By *COTTON MATHER.*

Publifhed by the Special Command of his EXCELLENCY the Go-venour of the Province of the *Maffachufetts-Bay* in *New-England.*

Printed firft, at *Bofton* in *New-England*; and Reprinted at *London*, for *John Dunton*, at the *Raven* in the *Poultry.* 1693.

The Ghost of
Sergeant Davies

The Clachan of Inverey, circa 1910

Devils in the Flesh

*Jacques Algarron
and Denise Labbé
arriving at the
court in Blois*

own plans, however stupid and savage they were. Why he killed his siblings is harder to fathom. To remove witnesses . . . or rivals for the family estate? As a final act of viciousness towards his parents? Or did he not wish them to survive, despising him?

On Monday, 18 November 1974, a grand jury in Riverhead, Suffolk County, brought in an indictment charging Ronnie with six counts of murder in the second degree.[1] As though to make the case even more like a modern morality play, at the same time 800 mourners were attending the funerals of the slain; many classmates of the three younger children were there, as were two former presidents of the New York City Patrolman's Benevolent Association, who were friends of the father; the six-mile procession to St Charles Cemetery, Pinelawn, had had an escort of nine Suffolk County motorcycle-policemen.

Ronnie did not come to trial until the fall of 1975. At a preliminary hearing in September 1975, he claimed that the one-murder confession had been beaten out of him by the police. He admitted to initialling statements and diagrams relating to his dumping of bloodstained clothes and cartridges in a Brooklyn sewer. Already he was demonstrating the crucial weakness in his defence. On the one hand, he was a victim of police brutality; on the other, his statements were true. This schizophrenic defence would lead his court-appointed lawyer, William Weber, to suggest that Ronnie was insane.

The trial, before State Supreme Court Justice Thomas Stark, took place at Riverhead and lasted seven weeks. There were fifty witnesses and one hundred and fifty pieces of evidence. Testimony was given by convicts who had shared cells with the defendant, neighbours in Amityville, in-laws. Ronnie showed a chilling lack of remorse. He threatened an aunt who testified, as well as Gerald Sullivan, the assistant district attorney who prosecuted. The defence

---

1. In New York State, first-degree murder is reserved for the killing of police officers. It carries (in theory, if not in practice) the death penalty. The highest penalty for second-degree murder is life in prison with no chance of parole.

psychiatrist labelled him 'a paranoid psychotic who could not know it was wrong to kill his family'. The prosecution psychiatrist countered by saying that the defendant had 'an antisocial personality but could tell if his behaviour was right or wrong'.

According to the *New York Times*, the defence attorney did not materially help his client's case: the argumentative technique used by Mr Weber visibly irritated Justice Stark. Mr Weber claimed that Gerald Sullivan had omitted witnesses who would demolish the contention about the strongbox as the motive; he insisted that Ronnie had been denied his 'Miranda Right'.[1] None of this impressed the jury, and it may be wondered if it really impressed Mr Weber. The *New York Times* quoted him as saying: 'I'm getting more out of this from the publicity.'

On 19 November 1975, the jury was charged by Justice Stark. Two days later, they returned a verdict of Guilty on all six counts. On 4 December, the judge sentenced Ronnie to life imprisonment. Weber made a much-publicised but unsuccessful appeal. The legal process may have occupied too long a while, but justice was finally done.

That is the undoubtedly true story that shook up Amityville. It is not, however, the story that made this suburban community world-famous.

A Man's Home

In one of his essays, Edmund Pearson wonders what happened to various criminals after their acquittal or imprisonment. Equally interesting is what has happened to the sites of famous crimes. Ford's Theatre, after a period of use as a government building, and partial destruction in 1893, has been rebuilt and turned into a memorial to Abraham Lincoln ... the home of Lizzie Borden is still a

1. The 'Miranda Right' stems from a decision of the Supreme Court in 1966 — basically that a suspect in a crime must be warned by police that he does not have to say anything, that what he says can be used against him, and that he has the right to a lawyer to advise him on his answers to questions.

home for someone in Fall River ... the house at Hopewell from which the Lindbergh baby was kidnapped is now a reformatory for boys ....

In the winter of 1975, a Mr George Lutz needed to find a new home. He was the owner of W.H. Parry, Inc, a surveying company begun by his grandfather, with offices at Syosset, Nassau County. He came from Deer Park, Suffolk County. He was married to Kathleen, née Connors, a divorcee with three children named Chris, Danny and Missy. They also had a dog called Harry. Though George Lutz had been looking for a house priced at around \$35,000, he was persuaded to purchase the \$80,000 former DeFeo home.

On Thursday, 18 December 1975, the Lutz family came with their belongings in a U-Haul Trailer – and with five friends who had offered to assist. Shortly after they started moving in, Father Frank Mancuso turned up. He, the local priest, knew Mrs Lutz and her children. She asked him to bless the house. Later on, he would claim that all day he 'felt funny'. He entered the house, flicked some holy water, and was about to make his blessing when a masculine voice said loudly: 'Get out!' Mancuso, alone at the time, finished the benedictions and left. On his way home, he very nearly had an automobile accident. A fellow-priest who accompanied him part of the way home soon afterwards really did have a bad crash. All very unsettling....

The Lutzes have hardly had time to settle in when unsettling things start happening to them. George Lutz becomes sullen – and also, one surmises, at times rather whiffy, for he refuses to wash for days on end. He lets his hair grow, his unprecedented beard as well – so that (as he learns later) he looks uncannily like Ronnie DeFeo Jr. For no apparent reason, his two stepsons have several fights. Missy says that she has a new friend, a pig named Jodie. One night when George is outside, he sees a pig staring with beady red eyes through Missy's window. He keeps waking up every night, always dead on 3.15am (which something, or someone, tells him is when the DeFeo

91

murders occurred); he looks at his sleeping wife and notices that she has become a toothless hag; one night she levitates, and he needs all his strength to pull her down. Green slime oozes from certain walls ... the bowls of the toilets turn black, and the house-proud Kathleen has to scrub and scrub to get them fairly clean ... the basement gives off an overpowering stench of excreta ... doors securely locked at night are off their hinges next morning ... a brass-band disturbs George every night (whether it is the martial music that wakes him regularly at 3.15 is impossible to determine).

The Lutzes do not suffer alone. On his way to his wedding, Kathleen's brother stops at the house to pick up the family; he leaves $1500 in an envelope in his coat, and the envelope disappears. Visitors to the house get the shivers from an unpleasant aura (or 'karma', as the aura subsequently gets to be called). When Father Mancuso tries to phone the family, he hears nothing but static. He develops nasty blistering all over his body, and his temperature rises well above the norm. When he puts the family out of his mind, he gets well — but ill again the minute he shows concern for them. Like the basement of the Lutzes' house, parts of the Father's house give off a stink.

George Lutz begins to study the history of the house. He reads the reports on the trial. He learns that the site of the house was once a compound-cum-graveyard for dying or insane Indians; that one of the first white settlers in the area was a man named John Cathum or Ketchem, who had an evil reputation, perhaps at least partly because he hailed from Salem, Massachusetts. Quite by chance, apparently, he uncovers a hidden room, and then hears a rumour that Ronnie Jr used just such a room for animal sacrifices, possibly of pigs. He starts reading up on paranormal experiences and demonology. After learning that haunted houses are often found to be built over open cisterns (by which, according to one theory, evil spirits enter the houses), he happens upon just such an opening under the front steps.

Father Mancuso, having also considered demonic possession, gets his Bishop to allow the Lutzes to contact specialists in the paranormal. They pick the Psychical Research Institute in Durham, North Carolina – but before the investigators turn up, the family suffers from a nerve-racking localised storm and further experiences of what they are by now convinced are psychic phenomena, and on 14 January 1976, just twenty-eight days after arriving, they flee 112 Ocean Avenue.

One Man's Meat

'Poltergeist' is a German word meaning 'racketing spirit'. It refers to phenomena in or around a building that cannot be explained by the normal laws of science. A 'governing intelligence' is supposed to be evident from certain repeated activities of the poltergeist. There are accounts of such phenomena over the centuries. Making a mockery of the word 'proof', evidence questioning the accuracy of the accounts is ignored, discounted or denied by dedicated believers in the paranormal.

According to D. Scott Rogo, in *The Poltergeist Experience*[1], the key to the phenomena is 'PK' – standing for 'psychokinesis', an energy-source emanating from the brain of a person, usually a young one, that is stimulated by sexual restraints or repression imposed by elders. The destructive force often associated with poltergeists is due to 'emotional revolt'. This force can be limited to stone-throwing or noise-making; but it can get very serious, even life-threatening – sometimes it is manifested in furniture-breakage, sudden fires, or damage to automobile engines.

The incidents that plagued the Lutzes and Father Mancuso are thought by some to mingle the poltergeist with demonology. The central idea seems to be that whatever caused the Lutzes to move out of 112 Ocean Avenue must have influenced the previous residents – ie it

1. Penguin, London, 1979.

caused Ronnie DeFeo Jr to slaughter his family. In some written accounts of the Lutzes' experiences, it is mentioned in passing that Ronnie's lawyer, William Weber, took a deep interest in the theory, and began to fashion an appeal based on the influencing activities of demons on his client, but then, for some reason, decided not to pursue the idea.

You will have gathered that, so far as demons and things are concerned, I am a sceptic. I certainly don't feel that everything about our world, let alone any others, is understood, or even that such understanding will be achieved within the next two or three millennia. But, as I have implied, there seem always to be equivocal points in accounts of the paranormal. Accounts of what happened to and in the vicinity of the Lutzes while they were at 112 Ocean Avenue, Amityville, are peppered with them.

I have only outlined the Lutzes' adventures. Anyone wanting every single detail of every single incident should find Jay Anson's *The Amityville Horror*[1]. It is an easy read. Anson had earned his living as a writer of screen documentaries, mostly for television, and his book seems to have been designed so as to be easily turned into a screen-play. There are many problems with the story of the Lutzes which are not fully considered in the book (the copyright of which, incidentally, was shared by Anson and the Lutz family; Father Mancuso contributed an introduction).

According to the book, a brief comment made by a house-broker to George Lutz was, it seems, the only thing he had ever heard about the DeFeo tragedy before he bought the house. But it seems unlikely. The family moved there from Deer Park, in Suffolk County, which is the county in which Amityville is situated ... the trial of Ronnie Jr was the longest in the history of Suffolk County, and the jury reached its verdict in November 1975 ... Ronnie was sentenced just a fortnight before the Lutzes moved into the house ...

1. Bantam, New York 1977.

Some of the phenomena seem rather *un*strange. Several times, noises in the night caused George to go downstairs – and he was amazed that Harry the dog was sound asleep each time. Granted that dogs are supposed to stir when there are noises in the night, but on each of those occasions no human but George heard the noise; everyone other than George was asleep – and were not even woken by his downstairs investigating. This surely suggests that maybe there was no noise at all – that he imagined or dreamt one. Later on, the others claimed that they experienced various nocturnal phenomena – but then it was only when they were all wandering sleepy-eyed around the house that Harry bothered to get up as well.

The smell of excreta (specified by the Lutzes and by Father Mancuso as being of the human kind) has a significance that is lost on people who are not versed in demonology. I should explain for their benefit that Satan's presence is supposed to be revealed by such a smell. Therefore we are to conclude that all the troubles were caused by The Evil One. Well, maybe . . . but one does feel that that conclusion should have been verified – perhaps by a spare-time psychic who was a full-time sanitation engineer?

There was criticism of the phenomenon from the start. In the *Washington Post Book World*, Curt Surplee raised doubts about the authenticity of aspects of the story; he had looked into the so-called history of the property, and learned, he said, that the Shinnecock Indians, indigenous to the Amityville area before the white settlers arrived, never had an enclosure for the sick or mad or dying or dead *anywhere*, let alone on or anywhere near where 112 Ocean Avenue now stood.

Pete Stevenson, a reporter for *The Morning Call* of Allentown, Pennsylvania, checked up on an incident related in the book – a visit by an Amityville police sergeant, during which he observed that a door had been ripped off the boat-house and that there were pig-tracks outside the house (made by Missy Lutz's paranormal pet?)

Though the Lutzes had flown by the time that investigators for the Psychical Research Institute arrived at the house, a television company got them to conduct a seance there; they detected no sign of activity, supernatural or otherwise.

The film version of Anson's book, starring James Brolin as George and Rod Steiger as Father Mancuso, opened to mixed reviews in 1979. Janet Maslin, writing in the *New York Times*, awarded it 'a definite B-minus', saying of Steiger that 'he bellows and weeps and overdoes absolutely everything'. The last of those criticisms of Mr Steiger's performance might also be levelled at most of the accounts of 'the Lutz phenomena' written by people determined in their belief that the tale is true.

A Last Angry Man

Imagine that you are in the neigbourhood of what used to be 10 Rillington Place, West London; you tag on to a crowd of people who are watching a plaque being fixed to the structure that now occupies that spot. While still at the edge of the crowd, you wonder if the plaque notes the possible miscarriage of justice in the trial and execution of Timothy Evans, or if it is a memorial to Christie's several undoubted victims. Having edged your way through the crowd, you read the following:

> On this site, in the year of Our Lord 1347 AD,
> stood the residence of Jasper Honeythumber, Esquire,
> who, when requested by His Lordship, the Lord
> Chancellor, to devise a means of raising the Royal
> Exchequer's Funds, was inspired to invent Graduated
> Income Tax.
>
> Dedicated this day [whatever it is] by
> The Civil Service Association.

Considering the very real tragedy of the women who were killed by Christie, and the possibility of a miscarriage of justice in the Evans case, you would, I believe, feel outraged that the site was being commemorated for the reason given on the plaque.

Well, 112 Ocean Avenue, Amityville, is famous now, just like 10 Rillington Place, West London. There is a similarity in the number of victims at each location. But the fame — or should I say infamy? — of the Long Island address is all because of the so-called supernatural happenings after the DeFeo Massacre — and this writer is outraged at that. The real tragedy, the real Amityville Horror, has been shoved aside in favour of nocturnal marching-bands, green blancmange going globbedy-globbedy as it oozes through walls, a thunder-storm in a living-room, a little pig named Jodie that needs treatment for conjunctivitis.

The fact that the house has been inhabited by an apparently still-happy family for some years indicates, at the very least, that whatever gave the Lutzes such a torrid time must have exhausted itself in the process. Did Jay Anson ever believe much of the story, one wonders? He never spoke about what he did or did not believe. Maybe he comforted himself with the thought that the story, far from harming anyone, brought enjoyment to some — after all, Ronnie Jr was safely tucked away in jail, none of the other DeFeos could complain, and the Lutz family, now safe and sound in California, got a share of the proceeds.

Let us — please; even for God's sake — get back to the real tragedy: the tragedy of a family named DeFeo. Ronald and Louise DeFeo 'made it' — in terms of living in a pleasant community, receiving a good income, and having four nice kids. But they had one kid who was lousy because they had failed to bring him up sensibly. I have no doubt that they loved young Ronnie — and little doubt that if they had been less anxious to get his love in return, they would have taken cruel-to-be-kind actions that might well have averted the tragedy. When the police arrested Ronnie for stealing the outboard-motor, when he was caught using drugs, when he lied about the money stolen from the auto dealership — each time his parents tried to save him from the punishment he *needed*. When, at last, they presented him with an ultimatum to reform or be thrown out, it was too late. The lousy kid had turned into a senseless egotist who much preferred to destroy those who loved him than to risk losing his comfort. His egotism strengthened his belief — based on experience — that he could commit crimes, *any* crimes, and get away with them.

The Ghost of Sergeant Davies

WILLIAM ROUGHEAD

'You must not tell us what the soldier or any
other man said, Sir; it's not evidence.'
BARDELL *v* PICKWICK

FEW JUDICIAL UTTERANCES are better known or
more widely quoted than this immortal dictum of Mr
Justice Stareleigh. Yet there was precedent against his
Lordship's ruling, for in the year 1754 the High Court of
Justiciary at Edinburgh had admitted as evidence what was
said by 'the soldier's' ghost! and so lately as 1831 the
testimony of a voice from the other world was accepted in
the Assynt murder case by the same tribunal. But English
practice was no stricter, and although only two instances of
spectral evidence occur in the State Trials, the research of
Mr Andrew Lang has disclosed similar cases. Both of the
Scots spirits spoke in Gaelic, which would seem to be an
appropriate medium of communication but for the fact
that the soldier, an Englishman, while in the flesh had no
knowledge of that tongue.

The case first mentioned arose out of the slaying of
Sergeant Davies, and the trial of his murderers was
privately printed for the Bannatyne Club at the instance of
Sir Walter Scott. The time was some three years after the
doleful day of Drummossie, the place a solitary hillside at
the head of Glenclunie, in the heart of the Grampians. 'A
more waste tract of mountain and bog, rocks and ravines,
extending from Dubrach to Glenshee, without habitations

of any kind until you reach Glenclunie, is scarce to be met with in Scotland,' writes Sir Walter; 'a more fit locality, therefore, for a deed of murder could hardly be pointed out, nor one which could tend more to agitate superstitious feelings.'

The swell following the great gale of the 1745 Rebellion had not subsided in the remoter Highlands; and bands of disaffected and broken men still lurked in security among the grim defiles and rugged fastnesses of that formidable land. The disarming of the Highlanders was a farce, as Prestongrange admitted to David Balfour. To stamp out the smouldering embers of the Rising, and to enforce the Disarming Act and that which proscribed the national dress, the Government still maintained garrisons throughout the suspected districts. From these stations small pickets were sent out to occupy various posts, whence they communicated with one another, and constantly patrolled the country.

In the month of September, 1749, Sergeant Arthur Davies, with a party of eight men of the regiment of foot commanded by Lieutenant-General Guise, were quartered at Dubrach, a small upland farm near the clachan of Inverey in Braemar. They had marched thither in the previous June from their headquarters at Aberdeen. Another party of the same regiment, under the command of a corporal, guarded the Spittal of Glenshee, some eight miles off. In the course of patrolling the district, these two parties were wont to meet twice a week at a spot midway between their respective stations. During the three or four months in which Sergeant Davies had occupied the hostile territory, he seems to have discharged his onerous duties with tact and moderation, and though officially unpopular, had managed to obtain the goodwill of his subject neighbours. The private tastes and character of the man were likeable: he was of a genial disposition, a keen and indefatigable sportsman, fearless, thrifty, and particular in his dress. For one in his position, his circumstances were prosperous. He had been married for about a year to the widow of a former comrade, and his wife shared the responsibilities of his post. Beyond Dubrach and farther up

Strathdee there was at that time no cultivated land, and it was the sergeant's daily custom, combining business and pleasure, to wander by himself with rod or gun among the hills, glens, and streams of those inhospitable and lonely wilds. Though often warned of the risk to which such habits exposed him at the hands of lawless and desperate men, many of whom were then 'in the heather', the sergeant laughed at danger, and continued to 'gang his ain gait'.

His figure was a notable one in so poor a neighbourhood. His ordinary dress was 'a blue surtout coat, with a striped silk vest, teiken breeches, and brown stockings'. He carried a green silk purse containing his little capital, fifteen and a half guineas in gold, and a leather purse with silver for current expenses. The existence of this green silk purse was a matter of common knowledge, for it was his kindly way, when playing with the children of the clachan, 'to rattle it for their diversion'. He wore two gold rings, one plain, engraved on the inside with the letters D.H. and the motto, 'When this you see, Remember me.' This 'posie' had reference to the late David Holland, sometime paymaster of the regiment, and the sergeant's predecessor in the lawful affections of his spouse. It would appear that he had no sentiment in such matters, for his brogues were enriched with a pair of large silver shoe-buckles formerly the property, and also bearing the initials, of the defunct. The other ring, which plays a part in the story, was of curious design, and had 'a little lump of gold' in the form of a heart raised upon the bezel. The sergeant, further, wore silver buckles at his knees, a silver watch and seal at his fob, two dozen silver buttons on his waistcoat, and carried in his pocket a penknife of singular form. His 'dark-mouse-coloured hair' was tied behind with a black silk ribbon, and his silver-laced hat, with a silver button, had his own initials, misplaced, cut on the outside of the crown. A gun with a peculiar barrel, given to him by a brother officer, completed his usual equipment.

Thus accoutred and adorned, Sergeant Davies, very early

on the morning of Thursday, 28 September 1749, bade farewell to his wife at the house of Michael Farquharson, where they lodged, and set forth in advance of his men to meet the patrol from Glenshee. Four of his party followed him soon after. This arrangement was not unusual, and on the return journey he would often 'send the men home and follow his sport'. An hour after sunrise, he was seen and spoken to in Glenclunie by one John Growar, whom he had occasion to reprimand for wearing a coat of tartan, in contravention of the Act. With characteristic good-nature, Davies 'dismissed him, instead of making him prisoner'. The four soldiers from Dubrach duly met the corporal's guard from Glenshee; on their way they had a distant glimpse of the sergeant still pursuing his sport, and heard him fire a shot. They marched home in the afternoon without seeing anything further of him. After the patrols had separated, the Glenshee party encountered the sergeant at the Water of Benow, half a mile from the rendezvous. Davies informed the corporal 'that he was going to the hill to get a shot at the deer'. The corporal thought it 'very unreasonable in him' to venture on the hill alone, as he himself was nervous even when accompanied by his men. To which the sergeant answered 'that when he had his arms and ammunition about him, he did not fear any body he could meet'. Whereupon they parted company; and from that hour Sergeant Davies vanished from among living men, and his place knew him no more.

Next day the news spread throughout the district that the sergeant had disappeared. The captain of the garrison at Braemar Castle sent a party of men on the Sunday to Dubrach, and on the Monday the whole countryside was raised to search for the missing man. After four days of fruitless labour, the search was abandoned; no trace of the sergeant could be found. From the first, his wife was certain that he had met with foul play. As she afterwards said, 'It was generally known by all the neighbourhood that the sergeant was worth money and carried it about with him.' She scouted the rumour that he had deserted, 'for that he and she lived together in as great amity and love as any couple could do that ever was married, and that he never was in use to stay away a night from her; and that it was not possible he could be under any temptation to desert, as he was much esteemed and beloved by all his officers, and had good reason to believe he would have been promoted to the rank of sergeant-major upon the first vacancy.' Her view came to be the accepted one, and the opinion of the country was that the sergeant had been robbed and murdered, and his corpse concealed amid the desolate high places of the hills.

In June 1750, nine months after the disappearance, Donald Farquharson, the son of Michael, with whom Davies had lodged when on earth, received a message from one Alexander M'Pherson 'that he wanted much to speak to him'. M'Pherson was then at his master's sheiling (shepherd's hut) in Glenclunie, some two miles distant from Dubrach. A few days afterwards, Farquharson went to see him as requested, 'when M'Pherson told him that he was greatly troubled with an apparition, the ghost of the deceased Sergeant Davies, who insisted that he should bury his bones; and that he having declined to bury them, the ghost insisted that he should apply to Donald Farquharson, saying that he was sure he would help to bury his bones.' The spirit's confidence was misplaced, for Donald at first declined the office, and 'could not believe that M'Pherson had seen such an apparition'. But on the ghost-seer stating that, guided by his visitant's description, he had actually found the bones in question, and offering to take him to the spot, Donald reluctantly agreed to accompany him; 'which', as he naively says, 'he did the rather that he thought it might possibly be true, and if it was, he did not know but the apparition might trouble himself.'

M'Pherson led him to the Hill of Christie, between Glenchristie and Glenclunie, two or three miles from Dubrach, and about half a mile from the road taken by the patrols between that place and Glenshee. The body, which lay on the surface of the ground in a peat moss, was practically reduced to a skeleton. The bones were separated and 'scattered asunder', but the 'mouse-coloured' hair of the unhappy sergeant, still tied with the black silk ribbon, was intact. Fragments of blue cloth, some pieces of striped stuff, and a pair of brogues from which the tags for the buckles had been cut, left little doubt as to the identity of the remains.

M'Pherson told his companion that when he first found the bones, eight days before, they lay farther off under a bank, and 'he drew them out with his staff'. Donald enquired, 'If the apparition had given any orders about carrying his bones to a churchyard?' and learning that the spirit had indicated no preference for any specific resting-place, he agreed to bury the bones on the spot. They accordingly dug a hole in the moss with a spade brought by M'Pherson, and buried therein all that they had found.

Now, though M'Pherson does not appear to have told Farquharson at this time, he afterwards swore that the ghost, being pressed by him to disclose who had slain the sergeant, did, on the occasion of its second appearance, actually name the murderers. To this we shall return.

Between the discovery of the bones and the communication to Donald Farquharson, M'Pherson had informed John Growar (the man to whom the sergeant had spoken about the tartan coat) both of his spectral visitor and of what he had found. 'John bid him tell nothing of it, otherwise he would complain of him to John Shaw of Daldownie.' To anticipate this, M'Pherson himself reported the circumstance to Daldownie, who 'desired him to conceal the matter, and go and bury the body privately, as it would not be carried to a kirk unkent [unknown], and that the same might hurt the country, being under the suspicion of being a rebel country'. Later, M'Pherson showed Growar where he had found the bones. It was not far from the place at which John had met the sergeant on the day of his death.

Notwithstanding the desire for secrecy expressed by all the parties, someone let out the finding of the body, with

the result that local interest was directed to the Hill of
Christie. James Growar, a relative of John, presently found
there the sergeant's gun, and a girl named Isobel Ego picked
up a silver-laced hat with a silver button on it, afterwards
identified as his. Isobel, who had been sent by her master
to the hills to look for some horses, remarked on her
return, 'That she had come home richer than she went out',
and produced her find. Her mistress 'had no peace of mind,
believing it to be Sergeant Davies's hat, and desired it might
be put out of her sight'; so the farmer hid the hat under a
stone by the burnside, near his house, and knew no more
of it. Some time after, however, 'the bairns of Inverey',
playing about the burnside, lighted upon the hat and took
it to the village. It then passed successively through the
hands of Donald Downie, the miller of Inverey, and of
James Small, factor on the forfeited estate of Strowan, into
the custody of John Cook, barrack-master at Braemar
Castle, who four years later produced it at the trial. We
shall hear of the Strowan factor again.

The barrack-master afterwards said that within ten days
of the sergeant's disappearance, 'it was reported that he had
been murdered by two young men about Inverey'. By the
following summer, not only was the story of the ghostly
visitant and the resulting discovery of the bones well
known throughout the neighbourhood, but 'it was
clattered' that the spectre had denounced by name as the
murderers two persons then living in the district. These
were Duncan Terig, *alias* Clerk, and Alexander Bain
Macdonald. Both were men of questionable character, and
reputed thieves. Clerk lived with his father in Inverey
without visible means of livelihood, and Macdonald, who
was forester to Lord Braco (the first Earl Fife), resided in
Allanquoich. Apart from their supernatural impeachment,
many material facts confirmatory of their guilt
accumulated against them in the public mind, but four
years elapsed before they were brought to trial. It does not
appear from the official record how the tardy sword of
justice came to be drawn so long after the event, for not

until September 1753 were Clerk and Macdonald apprehended on the charge and committed to the Castle of Braemar. The Lord Advocate stated in Court that the prisoners 'were at last accused by the general voice of the country', and that the cause of delay in bringing them to trial was that 'at first the proof against them did not appear so pregnant'. But certain events after the trial throw some light, as we shall see, on how the charge was made.

On 23 January 1754, the prisoners, being judicially examined before Lords Strichen and Drummore, two of the Lords Commissioners of Justiciary, each gave different and contradictory accounts of their movements upon the day of the murder. Clerk declared that he, in company with Macdonald, was upon the Hill of Gleney the day Sergeant Davies disappeared; that both were armed with guns; that Macdonald fired one shot at some deer; and that at ten o'clock that morning he parted from Macdonald on the hill and returned to his father's house, to which Macdonald came the same evening, and where he stayed all night. Macdonald declared that he spent the night at his own house in Allanquoich, and did not see Clerk after they parted on the hill about nine or ten o'clock. For the rest, his declaration concurred with Clerk's.

The trial began before the High Court of Justiciary at Edinburgh on 10 June 1754, the judges being Lord Justice-Clerk Alva, who presided, and Lords Strichen, Drummore, Elchies, and Kilkerran. The two last named had assisted Argyll, the Justice-General, at the judicial murder of James of the Glens two years before, as immortalised by Stevenson. The Lord Advocate, William Grant of Prestongrange, so vividly portrayed in *Catriona*, Patrick Haldane and Alexander Home, 'His Majesties Solicitors', and Robert Dundas, conducted the prosecution. The prisoners were represented by Alexander Lockhart (who ten years later in that Court heroically defended Katharine Nairn) and Robert M'Intosh, the friend of Scott.

In the debate upon the relevancy, which, as was then usual, occupied the first day of the proceedings, it was argued for the panels that they were persons of good fame, and had no malice against the sergeant; that they had a true and warrantable cause for being on the hill under arms; and that they did so openly and avowedly. It was further objected that though arrested for the murder as already described, and having almost 'run their letters' without being served with an indictment, they were again committed for theft, and the time nearly expiring in that case also, they were detained on a third warrant for wearing the Highland Dress, and last of all, 'upon the malicious information of some private informer', were served with this indictment. They offered to prove that after they had left the hill, the sergeant was seen alive with his party, but in support of this allegation no shadow of evidence was afterwards adduced. The Lord Advocate confidently answered that such facts and circumstances would come out upon proof as would satisfy the jury of the panels' guilt. The delay complained of was owing to no intention of his to oppress the panels – 'he had early information of the murder charged upon and was very willing and desirous it might come to light' – but was due to the difficulty of obtaining conclusive evidence against them, which he hoped he had now done. The Court found the libel relevant, and adjourned till the following day.

At seven o'clock next morning (11 June), the trial was resumed, and a jury, composed of Edinburgh tradesmen, was empanelled. Macdonald was allowed to amend his declaration to the effect that he had spent the night of the murder at the house of Clerk's father in Inverey. The Lord Advocate's first witness was Jean Ghent, the widow of the murdered man, from whose evidence many of the foregoing facts have been related. She described the dress and belongings of her husband on that morning when she last saw him alive, and identified as his the hat and gun found on the hill, as already mentioned. She had seen him cut his initials on the hat, and had remarked to him at the time, 'You have made a pretty sort of work of it by having misplaced the letters.' The stock of the gun had been altered, but she knew it by 'a cross rent' in the middle of the barrel, occasioned, as her husband had told her, by his firing a shot when the gun was over-loaded. While the search-party was being organised, she had asked the prisoner Clerk, 'whom she took to be a particular friend, to try if he could find the body'! The poor woman then little knew how well qualified he was to do so.

Donald Farquharson, whose evidence we have recounted, told how M'Pherson communicated to him the spirit's message, and described the subsequent burial of the remains. He also identified the gun produced, having been present when Davies fired the charge which cracked the barrel. He had seen gold rings, 'one of which had a knob upon it', on the fingers of Elizabeth Downie, a girl whom Clerk had married since the murder. It struck him as being like the sergeant's ring, and he questioned her about it, but she said it had belonged to her mother. Macdonald, as Lord Braco's forester, was the only man who had a warrant 'for carrying guns for killing of deer', and Clerk was usually associated with him in his expeditions. Clerk was reputed a sheep-stealer. The witness knew nothing against Macdonald 'but that he once broke the chest of one Corbie, and took some money out of it'. He considered M'Pherson, the ghost-seer, 'an honest lad', but it was the general opinion 'that all is not to be believed that he says'.

Alexander M'Pherson was then called. In the earlier part of his examination he made no reference to the ghost, but merely stated that in the summer of 1750 he found, lying in a moss bank on the Hill of Christie, the bones of a human body, which at the time he believed to be that of Sergeant Davies. His description of the appearance of the remains agreed with that given by Farquharson. When first discovered, the body was partially concealed, and 'by the help of his staff he brought it out and laid it upon the plain ground, in doing whereof some of the bones were separated one from another'. He narrated his conversations on the subject with Growar, Daldownie, and Farquharson, described the burial of the bones, and gave the following account of his parleyings with the disembodied sergeant:

One night in June 1750, being then abed in his master's sheiling at Glenclunie, 'a vision appeared to him as of a man clad in blue', which he at first took to be 'a real living man', namely a brother of Donald Farquharson. The spirit, presumably unwilling to disturb the other sleepers, withdrew to the door of the hut, and M'Pherson arose and followed it outside, when it made the startling announcement, 'I am Sergeant Davies!' It added that, in the days of its flesh, it had been murdered on the Hill of Christie nearly a year before, minutely described the place where the body was hidden, and requested M'Pherson to arrange with Donald Farquharson for its interment. Notwithstanding the singular character of the interview, M'Pherson retained sufficient wit to inquire who had done the deed. The spectre made answer that if M'Pherson had not asked, it might have told him, but as he had, it could not. Perhaps to do so was contrary to ghostly etiquette. Thereupon the apparition vanished 'in the twinkling of an eye'. So exact were its directions as to the position of the body that M'Pherson 'went within a yard of the place where it lay upon his first going out'. Although this should have been an absolute guarantee of the ghost's good faith, M'Pherson did nothing further in the matter. A week later, at the same time and place, 'the vision again appeared, naked, and minded him to bury the body'. M'Pherson repeated his inquiry as to the identity of the murderer, and the spectre, having apparently laid aside its reticence with its raiment, at once replied, 'Duncan Clerk and Alexander Macdonald', and vanished as before. Both conversations were held in Gaelic, with which language the sergeant, when in life, was unfamiliar. Excepting Growar, Daldownie, and Farquharson, M'Pherson had told no one about the vision, nor did he tell the other folks in the sheiling at that time.

Some whisper of the spirit's purpose must have reached the ear of Duncan Clerk, for that autumn he repeatedly invited M'Pherson to enter his service. Clerk's circumstances had unaccountably improved of late. He had taken upon lease the farms of Craggan and Gleney, and was married to Elizabeth Downie, the damsel with the remarkable ring. At Martinmas, 1750, M'Pherson, yielding to his solicitations, became a member of his houshold. He noticed that his new master carried a long green silk purse, while his mistress wore a gold ring, 'with a plate on the outside of it in the form of a seal', both of which, he heard it reported, had belonged to the murdered man. One day when they were together on the hill, Duncan, 'spying a young cow', desired M'Pherson to shoot it. The latter refused to do so, and administered the moral reproof 'that it was such thoughts as these were in his heart when he murdered Sergeant Davies!' Duncan at first used 'angry expressions', but M'Pherson sticking to his point, he 'fell calm', desired him to keep the secret and he would be a brother to him, offered to help him to stock a farm when he took one, and gave him a promissory note for twenty pounds Scots 'to hold his tongue of what he knew of Sergeant Davies'. M'Pherson afterwards asked Duncan for payment of the note and, failing to obtain it, left his service. That M'Pherson did tackle his master about the murder is corroborated by John Growar, who reports a conversation between them on the subject, when Duncan, to deprecate exposure, pathetically remarked, 'What can you say of an unfortunate man?' After Clerk's arrest, his brother Donald 'solicited' M'Pherson to leave the country, 'that he might not give evidence', and offered him 'half of every penny Donald was worth' if he would bear false witness at the trial.

Whatever may be thought of M'Pherson's ghost story, it is supported by the testimony of Isobel M'Hardie, in whose sheiling the vision appeared. This lady, who missed the spirit on its first call, deponed that on the night in question she, along with her servants, was sleeping in the hut when she awoke and 'saw something naked come in at the door in a bowing posture'. From motives of either modesty or fear, 'she drew the clothes over her head', and unfortunately saw nothing further. Next morning she mentioned the matter to M'Pherson, who, having decided to comply with the ghost's request, assured her 'she might be easy, for that it would not trouble them any more'.

James Macdonald, of Allanquoich, stated that, having heard the rumour of the panels' guilt, he applied to Clerk's father-in-law, Alexander Downie, to know if it were true. Downie admitted that it was so, adding, 'What could his son-in-law do, since it was in his own defence?' Macdonald had seen upon Elizabeth Downie's finger after her marriage a gold ring, 'having a little knap upon it like unto a seal', which he suspected had belonged to Davies. Peter M'Nab, a neighbour, also saw the gold ring, 'pretty massy, having a lump upon it pretty large', and asked Elizabeth how she came by it, to which she answered 'that she had bought it from one James Lauder, a merchant'. Elspeth Macara, Clerk's servant, had often seen her mistress wearing a gold ring 'with a knob upon it of the same metal'.

Lauchlan M'Intosh, who had been a servant of the sergeant's landlord, deponed that, some two years after the disappearance, he saw in the hand of the prisoner Macdonald a penknife resembling one Davies used to carry, which had certain peculiarities known to the witness. He remarked at the time that it was 'very like Sergeant Davies's penknife', but Macdonald merely observed 'that there were many sic-likes'.

John Grant, of Altalaat, deponed that the panels lodged in his house on the night of 27 September 1749, that preceding the murder. Next morning, 'after the sun-rising', they went out, each with a gun, saying 'that they intended to go a deer-hunting'. As he left home that morning to attend a fair at Kirkmichael, and did not return for four days, Grant knew no more of their doings. He was corroborated by his son, who saw the panels start on their shooting expedition, going up the water to the Hill of Gleney, a mile and a half from the Hill of Christie. Clerk was wearing a grey plaid. Jean Davidson, of Inverey, stated that, 'about sun-setting' on the day Sergeant Davies disappeared, she saw Clerk, 'having a plaid upon him with a good deal of red in it', return from the hill to his father's house in the clachan.

John Brown, ground-officer of Inverey, said that when, by order of the chamberlain, he called out the inhabitants to search for the missing sergeant, Clerk 'challenged him for troubling the country-people with such an errand, and upon this the witness and the said Duncan had some scolding words'.

Such was the circumstantial evidence adduced in support of the charge; but the Crown was in a position to prove by the direct testimony of an eye-witness that Davies undoubtedly met his death at the prisoners' hands. Angus Cameron, a Rannoch man, swore that upon the day of the murder he and a companion named Duncan Cameron, who had since died, were hiding, for political reasons, in the heather. They had spent the previous night on Glenbruar Braes, and were then lying concealed in a little hollow upon the side of the Hill of Galcharn on the look-out for one Donald Cameron, 'who was afterwards hanged', and some other friends from Lochaber, with whom they expected to foregather that day. They had lain there since 'two hours after sun-rising'. The time hung heavily enough upon their hands, and they would welcome any passing incident as a relief to the tedium of their vigil. About mid-day they observed Duncan Clerk, whom Angus knew by sight, and another man 'of a lower stature,' unknown to him, both with guns, pass the hollow where they lay. Clerk had on a grey plaid 'with some red in it'. An hour or so before sunset, Angus saw a man in a blue coat with a gun in his hand, whose hat was edged with white or silver lace, about a gun-shot off upon a hill opposite to the place where he lay. Coming up the hill towards the stranger were the two men he had seen in the morning. The three met upon the top of the hill, and after standing some time together Clerk struck the man in blue upon the breast, whereupon the man cried out, clapped his hand to his breast, 'turned about, and went off'. The other two 'stood still for a little', and then each of them raised his gun and fired at him practically at the same moment, though Angus could distinguish the separate reports. 'Immediately upon them, the man in blue fell.' The murderers then approached their victim, and the watcher saw them stoop down 'and handle his body'. While they were so employed, Angus and his companion deemed it prudent to beat a retreat, which they did unobserved, and, without waiting for their companions, left the district.

Not till the following summer did Angus chance to hear of the vanishing of Sergeant Davies, and realise that he had been present at his slaying. Hitherto he had told no one of what he had seen, but he now consulted two Cameron friends as to how, in the circumstances, he ought to act. They advised him to do nothing in the matter, 'as it might get ill-will to himself and bring trouble on the country'. The two Camerons above mentioned corroborated. When informed by Angus that he had seen Clerk and another shoot a man dressed 'like a gentleman or an officer' upon a hill in Braemar, one prudently said he did not want to hear any more on that subject, and the other that it would never do to have such a report raised of the country, and advised Angus 'to keep the thing secret'. We have already seen how the fear of possible reprisals had sealed the lips of those who long before could have enabled the authorities to bring the murderers to justice.

This concluded the evidence for the prosecution, which we have been particular in setting forth in view of the startling verdict thereon arrived at by the jury. The proof in exculpation consisted of the testimony of but three witnesses. Colonel Forbes of the town of New deponed that as justice of the peace he had been instructed to examine Elizabeth Downie (who, being Clerk's wife, was incompetent as a witness upon his trial), touching the nature and extent of her jewellery. She informed him that she was married to Clerk in harvest, 1751; that before her marriage she had a copper ring 'with a round knot of the same metal on it', which she gave to a glen-herd named Reoch; that since her marriage she had only possessed two rings, a small brass one, which she produced, and a gold one, which she got from her mother. It will be remembered that to other witnesses Elizabeth had given different and contradictory accounts of her rings. Two witnesses who had been at the shearing in Gleney on the day of the murder said they had seen Clerk there alone about noon. Gleney is a mile farther up the water towards the hill than Inverey, and is about the same distance from Glenclunie. Both witnesses were very vague as to the hour, which they fixed with reference to their dinner, admittedly a movable feast.

Reoch, who doubtless had his own reasons for declining to testify concerning the ring with the knob on it, having failed to obey his citation as a witness, was fined one hundred merks, the Court inflicting a similar penalty upon another absenting witness. The jury were then enclosed, and the Court adjourned at four o'clock in the morning of 12 June, having sat for twenty-one consecutive hours. At six o'clock the same afternoon, the jury, 'all in one voice', found the panels not guilty of the crime libelled! The Court then 'assoilized' Clerk and Macdonald, and dismissed them from the bar.

This amazing conclusion was, one would think, more likely to offend the sergeant's 'perturbed spirit' than the disrespect previously shown to his bones; but whether or not he resented the verdict and troubled in consequence the peace of the jury, we have no means of knowing. It is highly probable that he had already, by his well-meant intervention, done much to frustrate the ends of justice and bring about his murderers' acquittal; for the supernatural element thus introduced was seized upon by the defence to cast ridicule on the Crown case, and so obscure the very material evidence of the panels' guilt. Robert M'Intosh, one of their counsel, told Scott that M'Pherson, in cross-examination, swore that the phantom spoke 'as good Gaelic as ever he heard in Lochaber'. 'Pretty well,' said M'Intosh, 'for the ghost of an English sergeant!' But this fact was surely less marvellous than the appearance of the spectre at all; in such matters *c'est le premier pas qui coûte*.

It was Sir Walter's opinion that M'Pherson arrived at his knowledge of the murder 'by ordinary means', and invented the machinery of the vision to obviate the odium attaching to informers. Such also was the view of Hill Burton, who thought Farquharson a party to the fraud. But this theory ignores the testimony of Isobel M'Hardie, and, as we shall find from contemporary evidence, neither of these men did in fact give the information upon which the prisoners were charged. Unless they had themselves seen the deed done or heard Angus Cameron's account of its doing, they knew no more than any of their neighbours, and it does not appear that Angus had then spoken. They certainly displayed little zeal to discover the authors of the crime, for M'Pherson, despite the revelation, took service with the murderer and remained a year in his employment, while Farquharson did nothing whatever in the matter.

The reader will recollect that upon the spirit's first appearance M'Pherson took it for 'a real living man, a brother of Donald Farquharson'. It would be interesting to learn more of this person; where, for instance, he was that night, what were his relations with the accused, and whether he had not himself discovered the remains. For it is much more likely that someone, either with a knowledge of the facts or from a desire to fix public suspicion upon Clerk and Macdonald, the reputed murderers, assumed the spectral rôle and successfully imposed upon the credulous shepherd lad, than that the latter would, in the circumstances, invent and swear to so ridiculous a tale. Mrs M'Hardie, on the second visitation, saw a naked figure enter the low door of the hut 'in a bowing posture', which is more suggestive of a physical than a psychic intruder. Whatever the Lord Advocate may have thought of M'Pherson's good faith, it is difficult to see how he could ever have expected the jury to swallow the ghost, but it may be (for the records of these old trials are confusing) that the spirit was judicially evoked by Lockhart in cross-examination. Probably, had M'Pherson and Farquharson confined themselves to the bones and left the murderers to be named by Cameron, who saw and knew them, a conviction would have been secured, for M'Intosh admitted to Scott that both the counsel and agent of the accused were convinced of their guilt.

It has been conjectured, in explanation of the inexplicable verdict, that the jury were Jacobites, and as such would be indisposed to deal very strictly in so trifling a matter as the removal of a superfluous English sergeant, but the fact that they were all Edinburgh tradesmen hardly encourages the supposition. 'The whole affair,' writes Mr Andrew Lang, 'is thoroughly characteristic of the Highlanders and of Scottish jurisprudence after Culloden, while the verdict of "Not Guilty" (when "Not Proven" would have been stretching a point) is evidence to the ''common sense'' of the eighteenth century.'

A curious incident, unnoticed by Scott and Hill Burton, which arose out of the trial, throws some light on the former proceedings, and is in itself sufficiently quaint to be recorded. On Friday, 14 June, two days after the accuseds' acquittal, Alexander Lockhart, their counsel, presented in his own behalf to the Lords of Justiciary a petition and complaint against James Small, late ensign of the Earl of Loudon's regiment, and then factor upon the forfeited estate of Strowan, whose name, it will be recalled, had been mentioned during the trial. According to the petition, Small was 'the person upon whose instigation' Clerk and Macdonald had been prosecuted. He had been 'extremely industrious in searching out witnesses against them', and it was alleged that not only did he examine and take declarations from the witnesses in private, but after they were cited to give evidence in Court he 'dealt with' some of them not to appear, and endeavoured to intimidate others who did not say 'such strong things' as he expected. These matters, said Lockhart, he had thought it his duty to bring to the notice of the Court and jury at the trial, which he had accordingly done. Small, resenting his observations, had, armed with a sword and attended by two men 'of very suspicious appearances', lain in wait for Lockhart in the Parliament Close that Friday morning. Upon the arrival of the advocate at his usual hour for attending court, Small rushed upon him, 'made a claught at the petitioner's nose', and raising his stick, 'which he shaked over the petitioner's head', made the somewhat superfluous remark that his action was intended as a public affront, which if Lockhart proposed to resent, 'he would be at no loss to find out where the said James Small lived'. The petitioner pointed out that no words of his could adequately represent 'the atrociousness of the injury' to the dignity of the Senators of the College of Justice and the Faculty of Advocates in general and to himself in particular resulting from such scandalous behaviour, and that in these circumstances he was induced to seek redress by summary complaint to the Court 'rather than in the way and manner suggested by James Small'. The Court granted warrant for the apprehension of the militant factor, and ordered his committal to the Tolbooth till the next sederunt [sitting].

Answers to Lockhart's petition were lodged by Small, who stated that he did not receive any information that Clerk and Macdonald were reputed the murderers until he was instructed to inquire into the case and, if possible, discover the criminals. In December 1753 he assisted the Sheriff-Substitute in making such an inquiry, when it appeared from the precognitions then taken that the accused were the guilty parties, and they were charged accordingly. Had he been called as a witness upon their trial, the objection might validly have been made 'that he had given partial counsel in the cause', but though his name was included in the Crown list, the point did not arise. Mr Lockhart, however, in his address, had gratuitously attacked him, with a view to 'blacken the petitioner in the most public manner and to fix upon him for ever the basest and worst of characters'. He (Small) had been actuated throughout solely by his duty as a good subject and his desire to see justice done, and the strictures of Lockhart upon his conduct, which were well and widely known, so 'grieved, vexed, and confounded him by turns' that he was provoked to treat his traducer in the manner set forth in the petition. He protested that in so doing he had intended no disrespect either to the Court or to the Faculty, and though his behaviour 'had not perhaps been altogether legal', he hoped the Court would consider his 'great and just provocation'.

Next day Small was brought to the bar of the High Court of Justiciary. The proceedings took place behind closed doors, and the parties were heard by their procurators. The Lords found that the prisoner had been guilty 'of a high contempt of this Court, and of a high injury to the Faculty of Advocates and to the complainer, Mr Alexander Lockhart', and approved of the means taken by the complainer to obtain redress. They ordained Small to be imprisoned in the Tolbooth till Wednesday the 19th, when he must apologise in Court to the injured parties, and find caution to keep the peace for one year, under a penalty of fifty pounds sterling. Lockhart was ordered 'not to resent the injury done to him in any other manner'.

On 19 June, Small again appeared in custody before the Lords, gave in his bond of caution, and having publicly begged the pardon of the Court, of the Dean and Faculty of Advocates, and of Mr Alexander Lockhart, was thereafter dismissed from the bar.

Thus was vindicated the outraged majesty of the law, which, if it had signally failed to avenge the slaying of the sergeant, despite the co-operation of his unquiet spirit, could at least see justice done to an advocate's nose.

Devils in the Flesh

❖❖❖

RAYNER HEPPENSTALL

ON 1 MAY 1954, at a dance in Rennes, a typist who worked two hundred miles away in Paris, home for the weekend, made the acquaintance of Jacques Algarron, a cadet from the Army school at Coëtquidan. The following weekend, they became lovers. Neither was a novice. Denise Labbé had an illegitimate child, a daughter aged two, Catherine, by a house-doctor at Lorient, with whom she had lived until his departure for Indo-China and whom she had refused to marry on his return. The child was farmed out with entirely respectable foster-parents, a retired nurse and her husband, in the western outer suburbs of Paris, where her mother visited her quite regularly on Sunday afternoons. Algarron had two illegitimate children, whose mothers seem to have borne him no ill will, though he had refused to marry either.

He was himself the illegitimate son of an elderly Army officer, and a much older half-brother of his had at the Liberation been sentenced to death as a collaborator but reprieved. He was twenty-four. Denise Labbé was four years older. Her father had been a postman, who committed suicide in August 1940, throwing himself in the canal one Sunday morning when his daughter was fourteen. Her mother was still alive and lived in Rennes, where Denise still had friends. An intelligent and an industrious girl, she had received little formal education, and the only 'intellectual' connections she had were those she had made by promiscuous frequentation of university

119

circles in Rennes. Despite his illegitimacy, Algarron's background was bourgeois, and for a while he had attended a very good school indeed, Louis-le-Grand. Frequenting the bars and cellars of St Germain des Prés, he had picked up the jargon and read some of the fashionable 'anti-morality' books, particulary those by André Gide and would philosophise in a pretentiously half-baked manner which no doubt impressed his girls. It impressed Denise, that is certain. She was not at all bad-looking; round-faced, with a nice figure. Both were fair in colouring, he the more so. He had green eyes and was faunlike, with a nasty slit of a mouth.

He clawed and bit her, and she liked it. They even bought a penknife. On her summer holidays, with her mother and little Cathy, she proudly paraded her scars on the beach. He kissed the blood he drew and particularly enjoyed making love to her during her periods. He made her sleep with other men, though she did not want to. He thought that the human couple, to become a super-couple, ought to be united by something more than the pleasure of the senses, even with such sado-masochistic refinements. On 7 August, the day on which he passed out as an officer, as they rode in a taxi, he suggested killing the driver. But that would be a meaningless sacrifice. Her surest way of showing that she belonged wholly to him would be to kill her child. The suggestion was made and somewhat insisted on. By then, he had been posted to garrison duty with the gunners at Châlons-sur-Marne, and they met infrequently in Paris. She became pregnant, and he ordered her to have an abortion, which she did on the cheap and badly, so that curettage was needed.

On 22 September, she held Catherine over the balcony of her mother's second-floor premises in Rennes, but had not the heart to force the clinging fingers loose. A week later, she dropped the child into the canal from an iron bridge, but the child's clothes kept her afloat and she was rescued. On Saturday, 16 October, Cathy was found blue with cold in a stream near the foster-parents' home. In early November, Denise Labbé took her daughter to stay in

Vendôme with her sister and brother-in-law, a shady lawyer called Dusser. On the 8th, she held Cathy head-down in a vessel kept for washing clothes in the yard. At the funeral, suspicions were voiced by the foster-mother, but not until 6 December was Denise Labbé arrested. Presently, Jacques Algarron joined her at Blois, about a hundred miles south-west of Paris, charged under Article 60 of the Code Pénal, which deals with what we call accessories before the fact, 'those who, by gifts, promises, threats, abuse of authority or power, machinations or culpable artifices, shall have provoked the act or given instructions for it to be committed'. The original charge against Denise Labbé had, it may be noted, been under Article 63, for 'non-assistance to a person in danger'. Under our law, this is not a criminal offence. We may think it should be. That it is not may, at least, cause us to miss the point of such literary works, well-known and greatly admired in translation, as *The Fall* by Albert Camus. The lawyer in that book is guilty of a criminal offence under French law. It is not mere self-contempt which has led him to take refuge in Amsterdam.

In the days before the contraceptive pill, it was one of the disabilities of women that only the chaste, the careful, the undesired and the abnormal could be sure of avoiding unwanted pregnancy, the abrupt termination of which, whether by miscarriage, abortion or parturition, might induce a state of emotional disturbance verging, if not on madness, at least on diminished responsibility. This has sometimes been recognised in English law, in cases of infanticide by the mother. No doubt, among other factors, Denise Labbé's personality had been somewhat disturbed by her bungled abortion and its after-effects.

The trial of Denise Labbé and Jacques Algarron opened at Blois on Wednesday, 30 May 1956, in a thunderstorm, which rose to its height while the clerk to the court was reading the indictment, and briefly extinguished the lights, so that for a while the courtroom was illuminated only by flashes of lightning at the windows.

The president of the court was M. Lecocq, bespectacled, white-moustached, gentle in manner. Of the two assessors, M. Sorlin, on his left, seemed too young for his place, and on his right sat a good-looking woman in her thirties, Mme Kopenski. Before them, on a broad dais, stood Exhibit A, the *lessiveuse* in which, eighteen months previously, Catherine Labbé, then aged two and a half, had been held head downward till she died. On to the dais from the wall to their right projected the little box in which sat M. Gay, *avocat-général*, for the prosecution. Beyond him was the dock and, in front of it, the bench and long desk for counsel for the defence, among whom were two very eminent Parisian barristers indeed: for Algarron, René Floriot; for Denise Labbé, a man of even greater if quieter distinction, Maurice Garçon, a member of the Académie Française, known as a writer on subjects commonly thought remote from jurisprudence and case-law, demonology for instance, which in fact did not seem remote that sultry afternoon.

Maître Floriot had two juniors. With Maître Garçon, a man of unusually narrow, clean-shaven face, his short grey hair parted in the middle, sat the leader of the Loir-et-Cher bar association, M. le Bâtonnier Simon, venerably white-bearded. The jury was all male, seven farmers. There was no shortage of journalists from Paris; but there were few distinguished visitors, at best a couple of actresses (resting at the height of the season) and two singers from the existentialist basements of St Germain des Prés, probably there less from general interest than to lend moral support to later witnesses, of whom several had been Algarron's girl-friends in those Left-Bank surroundings. Yet all France was interested in the case, none more so than such eminent writers as François Mauriac, Jean Cocteau, Jules Romains, André Breton, Jean Schlumberger and Marcel Jouhandeau, all of whom would have their say when it was over, Cocteau describing it as the case of the century.

Maître Garçon's first intervention was to ask whether his

client could be moved to the end of the dock, just behind himself and thus farther away from Algarron, at which Maître Floriot was heard to ask sarcastically whether the latter was expected to hypnotise Labbé in open court, with the solid figure of a gendarme between them, and two others in the dock. After consultation with his assessors, M. Lecocq allowed counsel's request.

It is not uncommon for accomplices on trial together to be found making every effort to place the main burden of guilt on each other. Here, the cases against and for the two defendants were at once of a different nature and diametrically opposed. Even in an English court, it seems unlikely that Denise Labbé would have pleaded guilty, but she admitted all the facts with which she was charged, claiming only that she had acted under improper influence strongly and persistently exerted, so that her guilt, if not indeed her responsibility, was diminished. Jacques Algarron admitted no more than a few idle words, not intended to lead to any practical result. It would be Maître Floriot's aim to show that there was really no case for his client to answer, the only evidence that could be brought against him being the allegations of his former mistress, a proven liar, and some few scraps of letters of ambiguous import. Maître Garçon, on the other hand, since nothing alleged against his client could be disproved, must go all out for the case against Algarron. M. Gay could play it which way he pleased, but, since the case against Labbé presented no difficulty, he might be expected to concentrate on that against Algarron.

Journalists, it may be noted, had long since dubbed the two '*les amants maudits de Vendôme*'. This introduced an error of fact into the popular conception of the matter. The murder of little Cathy had indeed been committed in Vendôme, but, apart from a very little at a seaside resort, the defendants, however accursed, damned or doomed they might be, had done all their love-making in Rennes or Paris.

Spirited during the preliminary inquiry, especially when confronted with her lover, Denise Labbé, in a shabby two-piece tailor-made and white blouse, a handkerchief screwed up in her hand, made a poor, depressed showing in court, breaking down and sobbing at Algarron's vicious interjections. He, on the other hand, though his articulation was indistinct, had an answer to every question. His manner was defiant to the point of insolence. It did him no good. M. Gay demanded sentences of death for her, of life imprisonment for him. After hearing what Maître Floriot, Maître Garçon and again, more briefly, Maître Floriot had to say, the jury awarded sentences of life imprisonment to Denise Labbé, twenty years to Jacques Algarron. In practice, it would probably turn out that his sentence was the longer.

Among the books which, as it came out in court, Algarron had lent his mistress was *Les Nourritures Terrestres* by André Gide. During the past five years, François Mauriac had made it plain that he derived consolation from the thought of Gide roasting in hell. In his *bloc-notes* in *Le Figaro Littéraire*, he seemed nevertheless to regret that his youthful hero and later foe had been transferred to another jurisdiction.

> On the evidence of a single person, his mistress, contradicted by that of all the other women he knew, Algarron has been held responsible for a crime which he did not commit but which he may have inspired, without being impelled thereto by any discoverable motive. If such a verdict were to create a precedent, there would be no reason to stop there and not to charge the writer who may have inspired the young man.

In the same paper, Jean Schlumberger considered that from no point of view could the mind be satisfied by such a verdict, while to André Breton it was hopeless to expect understanding from such down-to-earth jurors. A Catholic writer of no less orthodox piety than Mauriac, M. Stanislas Fumet, thought the verdict quite normal, there was nothing scandalous about it, and Jules Romains wrote:

> This verdict seems to me as rational as anybody

could wish. I have tried to imagine what were the thoughts and reactions of the jury: mine would have been much the same.... It does seem beyond doubt that works of literature named in the course of the trial exercised an influence on one of the characters in this drama and, through him, on the other. But that raises the vast question of the freedom of literature and the arts.

In another paper, the weekly *Arts*, Marcel Jouhandeau wrote:

It remains for us to wonder what will take place tonight or tomorrow, after the sight of this catastrophe, between those of the same age as Denise and Jacques, who are in love with each other, as Jacques and Denise thought they were.

How can they fail to cast a look of suspicion on each other, at the thought that some uncontrolled deed or word, though dictated by tenderness, may one day bring them into opposition and make them enemies eternally irreconcilable?....

The Hand of God or Somebody

JONATHAN GOODMAN

A WEEK AFTER the death of the hangman, William Marwood, in September 1883, the following notice appeared in the national press:

> In consequence of the numerous applications which have been received at the Home Office for an appointment to the place of public executioner, we are requested to state it is neither the right nor the duty of the Secretary of State to make any such appointments. There is no such office as that of public executioner appointed by the Government. The person charged with the execution of capital sentences is the Sheriff. It is the right and the duty of the Sheriff to employ and to pay a fitting person to carry out the sentence of the law.

Among the wrongly addressed applications were these:

> I, H— R—, of Trindley Colliery, County of Durham, 6 feet 1 inch in my stocking feet, 14 stone weight, 35 years of age, would like the office of public executioner, in place of the late Marwood, deceased. I would hang either brothers or sisters, or anyone else related to me, without fear or favour.
>
> *Signed* H— R—
> (his mark)

Dere Sir,
> I am waiting outside with a coil of rope, and should be glad to give you a personal proof of my method.

Sir,

... I have some knowledge of Anatomy, am an exceedingly strong man, and can command sang-froid under any circumstances. I have witnessed Executions among all nations; consequently, there is no fear of my getting sick at the right moment.

Sir,

... I beg to state that by trade I am a Barber, and that my age is 34, and also that helth and nerve is good. In my Line of Business as a Barber I have had some years of Great Experience in the Formation of the necks and windpipes of all kinds of people, and, therefore, I think that the Situation, if dear Sir, it will be your Pleasure to appoint Me, would be the means of my Fulfilling it to your full satisfaction. I can Refer you for my testimonials to several Manchester Gentlemen of High honer and Long Standing.

Deer Sur,

I am ankshus to be yure publick exechoner, and i hereby apply for the job. i am thurty yeres old, and am willing to hang one or two men for nothink, so as you will see how I handle the job. i am strong, brave, and fear no man, and i will hang anybody you like, to show how i can do it. i inclose photo.

Sir,

... I have at various times made some very successful experiments in the art of hanging (by means of life-size figures) with the view to making myself thoroughly proficient in the despatch of criminals, and I have no hesitation in saying that I believe my system would be the most expeditious, never failing, and most humane that has ever been adopted or that could possibly be used, as it has been my greatest study. My system of hanging is not a lingering death by strangulation, but instantaneous and painless, rendered so by a small appliance of my own for the instant severing of the spinal cord. I may say that I adopt a variety of drops, varying from 7ft 10½ins to 16ft 11³⁄₃₂ ins. I shall be glad to conduct a series of experiments under your personal inspection on the first batch of criminals for execution, that you may see for yourself the superiority of my system over that of all others.

All of those letters, and the hundred or so others that also shouldn't have been sent to the Home Office, were forwarded to the Guildhall, there to be added to the pile of a thousand or so correctly-addressed ones. The Sheriffs of London and Middlesex invited some thirty of the applicants to attend interviews, separately but all on the same morning, at the Old Bailey. Of those, seventeen turned up, making one of the strangest gatherings that the Old Bailey — a place often frequented by strange gatherings — had ever housed. Within two hours the seventeen hopefuls had been interviewed, three of them twice — which indicates that the least appealing of them shambled into the Sheriffs' presence and were instantly ordered out of it.

The short-listed three were James Berry, of Bradford, Yorkshire (who, straightway after his second interview, wrote home, saying that he had 'virtually' been offered the job and had 'agreed upon the price'); Jeremy Taylor, of Lincoln, a builder who claimed to have been 'very intimate with the late Mr Marwood'; and Bartholomew Binns, a coal-miner near his native-town of Gateshead.

The Sheriffs chose Binns — and soon wished they hadn't. Having bungled three of the first four jobs he was given, he turned up for the fifth too drunk to be allowed near the scaffold, and was fired. It was subsequently reported that 'Binns, piqued at his dismissal, obtained a wax figure and a small gibbet, and appeared at fairs, etc, etc, exhibiting in a booth the manner in which he had carried out the executions during his short tenure of office. The police soon put a stop to his disgraceful exhibitions, and Mr Binns dropped out of the public sight.'

In 1884, James Berry, so recently rejected, was instated. The long-standing executioner, William Calcraft, had in his youth made shoes; Marwood throughout his life had mended them; and the footwear association was continued by Berry, who, having spent most of his twenties as a

constable in the Bradford and West Riding police force, had
become a seller of shoes in someone else's shop — a job that
he did not give up till he felt secure as an executioner. Berry
was less poorly educated than his predecessors: his handwriting was legible, he read unstumblingly (demonstrating
that ability while conducting Methodist services as a lay-
preacher), and, as the following extract from his memoirs
shows, he was quite — only quite — good at sums:

> I was slightly acquainted with Mr Marwood before his
> death, and I had gained some particulars of his method
> from conversation with him; so that when I undertook
> my first execution [on 31 March 1884], at Edinburgh, I
> naturally worked upon his lines. This first commission
> was to execute Robert Vickers and William Innes, two
> miners, who were condemned to death for the murder of
> two gamekeepers. The respective weights were 10 stone
> 4lb and 9 stone 6 lb, and I gave them drops of 8ft 6in and
> 10ft respectively. In both cases death was instantaneous,
> and the prison surgeon gave me a testimonial to the effect
> that the execution was satisfactory in every respect.
>
> Upon this experience I based a table of weights and
> drops. Taking a man of 14 stone as basis, and giving
> him a drop of 8ft, which is what is thought necessary,
> I calculated that every half-stone lighter weight would
> require a two inches longer drop, and the full table as
> I entered it in my books at the time, stood as follows:

14 stone	8ft	0in
13½	8	2
13	8	4
12½	8	6
12	8	8
11½	8	10
11	9	0
10½	9	2
10	9	4
9½	9	6
9	9	8
8½	9	10
8	10	0

> This table I calculated for persons of what I might
> call 'average' build, but it could not by any means be
> rigidly adhered to with safety.

That last comment of Berry's was an understatement. By the start of 1886 his percentage of 'mishaps' — though slightly lower than Marwood's, and nowhere near Binns's seventy-five per cent — was considered by the Home Secretary to be high enough to warrant the appointment of a Departmental Committee, under the chairmanship of Lord Aberdare, its brief 'to inquire into the existing practice as to carrying out of sentences of death, and the causes which in several recent cases have led either to failure or to unseemly occurrences; and to consider and report what arrangements may be adopted (without altering the existing law) to ensure that all executions may be carried out in a becoming manner without risk of failure or miscarriage in any respect'. The Committee recommended, *inter alia*, that all scaffolds should be much alike and that the ropes should be of standard thickness and length, and proposed a 'scale of drops' that differed in some respects from the one worked out by Berry.

None of Berry's 'subjects' was as famous beforehand as was one of them, John Lee, afterwards — his fame being chiefly due to the fact that he was able to savour it. Lee, having been found guilty of the stabbing to death of Emma Keyse, the sixty-eight-year-old spinster for whom he had worked domestically in the suburb of Torquay called Babbacombe, was scheduled to die in Exeter Prison at eight o'clock on the morning of Monday, 23 February 1885. But, depending upon which way one looks at it — from Lee's point of view or from Berry's — things went miraculously right or embarrassingly wrong. Berry gave his version of the non-event in a replying letter, dated 4 March, to the Under-Sheriff of Devon (who seems to have confused him, perhaps by allotting thirty days to February, into writing *inst*, then *ult*, rather than *ult* twice):

Executioner's Office,
1 Bilton Place, City Road,
Bradford, Yorks

Re JOHN LEE

Sir,

In accordance with the request contained in your letter of
the 30th inst, I beg to say that on the morning of Friday,
the 20th ult, I travelled from Bradford to Bristol, and on the
morning of Saturday, the 21st, from Bristol to Exeter,
arriving at Exeter at 11.50 am, when I walked direct to the
County Gaol, and signed my name in your Gaol Register
Book at 12 o'clock exactly. I was shown to the Governor's
office, and arranged with him that I would go and dine and
return to the Gaol at 2.0 pm. I accordingly left the Gaol,
partook of dinner, and returned at 1.50 pm, when I was
shown to the bedroom allotted to me, which was an
officer's room in the new Hospital Ward. Shortly afterwards I made an inspection of the place of Execution. The
execution was to take place in a Coach-house in which the
Prison Van was usually kept.... Two Trap-doors were
placed in the floor of the Coach-house, which is flagged
with stone, and these doors cover a pit about 2 yards by 1½
yards across, and about 11 feet deep. On inspecting these
doors I found they were only about an inch thick, but to
have been constructed properly should have been three or
four inches thick. The ironwork of the doors was of a frail
kind, and much too weak for the purpose. There was a
lever to these doors, and it was placed near the top of them.
I pulled the lever and the doors dropped, the catches acting
all right. I had the doors raised, and tried the lever a second
time, when the catch again acted all right. The Governor
was watching me through the window of his office and saw
me try the doors. After the examination I went to him,
explained how I found the doors, and suggested to him that
for future executions new trap-doors should be made about
three times as thick as those then fixed. I also suggested that
a spring should be fixed in the Wall to hold the doors back
when they fell, so that no rebounding occurred, and that
the ironwork of the doors should be stronger. The

131

Governor said he would see to these matters in future. I retired to bed about 9.45 that night....

On the Monday morning I arose at 6.30, and was conducted from the Bedroom by a Warder, at 7.30, to the place of execution. Everything appeared to be as I had left it on the Saturday afternoon. I fixed the rope in my ordinary manner, and placed everything in readiness. I did not try the Trap-doors as they appeared to be just as I had left them. It had rained heavily during the nights of Saturday and Sunday. About four minutes to eight o'clock, I was conducted by the Governor to the Condemned Cell and introduced to John Lee. I proceeded at once to pinion him, which was done in the usual manner, and then gave a signal to the Governor that I was ready.

The procession was formed, headed by the Governor, the Chief Warder, and the Chaplain followed by Lee. I walked behind Lee and six or eight warders came after me. On reaching the place of execution I found you were there with the Prison Surgeon. Lee was at once placed upon the trap-doors. I pinioned his legs, pulled down the white cap, adjusted the Rope, stepped to one side, and drew the lever – but the trap-door did not fall. I had previously stood upon the doors and thought they would fall quite easily. I unloosed the strap from his legs, took the rope from his neck, removed the White Cap, and took Lee away into an adjoining room until I made an examination of the doors. I worked the lever after Lee had been taken off, drew it, and the doors fell easily. With the assistance of the warders the doors were pulled up, and the lever drawn a second time, when the doors again fell easily. Lee was then brought from the adjoining room, placed in position, the cap and rope adjusted, but when I again pulled the lever it did not act, and in trying to force it the lever was slightly strained. Lee was then taken off a second time and conducted to the adjoining room.

It was suggested to me that the woodwork fitted too tightly in the centre of the doors, and one of the warders fetched an axe and another a plane. I again tried the lever but it did not act. A piece of wood was then sawn off one of the doors close to where the iron catches were, and by the aid of an iron crowbar the catches were knocked off, and the doors fell down. You then gave orders that the execution should not be proceeded with until you had communicated with the Home Secretary, and Lee was taken back to the Condemned Cell. I am of opinion that the ironwork catches of the trap-doors were not strong enough for the purpose, that the woodwork of the doors should have been about three or four times as heavy, and with ironwork to correspond, so that when a man of Lee's weight was placed upon the doors the iron catches would not have become locked, as I feel sure they did on this occasion, but would respond readily. So far as I am concerned, everything was performed in a careful manner, and had the iron and woodwork been sufficiently strong, the execution would have been satisfactorily accomplished.

I am, Sir,
Your obedient Servant,
JAMES BERRY

Henry M. James, Esq.,
Under-Sheriff of Devon,
The Close, Exeter

As likely an explanation for the failure of the apparatus appears in a book entitled *In the Light of the Law* (London, 1931), the author of which, Ernest Bowen-Rowlands, quotes a letter from a 'well-known person' who claimed to have heard from someone that

an old lag in the gaol confessed to him (I think when dying) that he was responsible for the failure of the drop to work in the execution of the Babbacombe murderer. It appears that in those days it was the practice to have the scaffold erected by some joiner or carpenter from among the prisoners. The man inserted a wedge which prevented the drop from working and when called in as an expert he removed the wedge and demonstrated the smooth working of the drop, only to re-insert it before Lee was again placed on the trap. This happened three times [*only twice, according to Berry*] and finally Lee was returned to his cell with doubtless a very stiff neck.

London
England,
Monday 16th.

Sir:

Having received your letter transferred from B'ford, stating that you will issue a summons for my attendance at Cork on the 20th inst. I beg to state that the Doctor gave his evidence in a straight-forward manner and the dep'y Governor (Oxford and the warders witnessed the Execution as well and as regards whit being my duty I do not shirk from my duty at all as it is not necessary for me to give evidence in such cases. I never do except when there is an accident occurs. If you like to send me a subpoena and the money to pay my first class expenses to Cork and back I will come if it will gratify your curiosity. If I do come I cannot tell you any more than what the Doctor has told you and perhaps not has much. But I am not at all proud if you send me the money to come with I shall be delighted with the second visit to Cork.,

Yours truly,

J. Berry

Berry's failure to hang Lee was the most markedly imperfect of his several imperfect performances. Three years after that debacle, on Tuesday, 10 January 1888, a superstition that he had inherited from his predecessor, William Marwood — that it was bad luck on someone, presumably other than a convicted murderer, for a murderer to be hanged when he was facing east — caused a breach of executional etiquette in the despatching of Philip Cross, an Army surgeon retired to the south of Ireland, who had used arsenic to murder his wife so as to be free to marry Effie Skinner, the governess of two of his five children. When Cross was brought to the gallows in Cork Prison, he insisted on facing the Governor and the rest of the witnesses, all of whom he knew socially — and who

*were gathered to the east of him. After two or three attempts
to get him facing in any other direction, Berry scolded him:
'This just won't do, Dr Cross — you have to die facing the
same way as anyone else.' He turned him north or south;
Cross at once turned back to the east; the Governor, not
knowing what all the directional fuss was about, exclaimed:
'Leave the doctor alone' — and Berry, cross himself by now,
didn't wait for the chaplain to say anything before pulling the
lever, letting Cross down with a lurch, and giving the
chaplain, left teetering on the brink, a nasty shock. Not till
the subsequent inquest, when the coroner said that he wanted
to question Berry about his pre-prayer pulling of the lever, was
it learned that he, with his wife and two minding detectives,
had gone off in a huff. There was 'something of a brawl'
between the coroner and the attending Deputy-Governor, a
Mr Oxford, in which members of the jury who wanted Home
Rule for Ireland joined in, and the inquest was adjourned till
the next day — when, despite the prison surgeon's reminder
that Cross could not be buried while the inquest was 'in
continuance', the coroner insisted that Berry be brought back
from England, and adjourned the inquest indefinitely. A letter
sent to Berry's home in Bradford was posted on to where he
was staying in London, and he retaliated with the letter
reproduced above (its grammatical and spelling errors indicate
that the letter to the Under-Sheriff of Devon re John Lee [page
131] was either composed on Berry's behalf or copy-edited
prior to its publication). The Governor had no power to issue
a 'supeona', and no wish to increase the cost of the execution
by paying Berry a second lot of 'First Class Expenses to Cork
and Back'. Though the Lord Lieutenant eventually gave an
order for the burial, the inquest remained adjourned — and is
still adjourned . . . which means that Dr Philip Cross, hanged
impatiently more than a century ago, is, in the eyes of the
law, not yet deceased.*

There is, I must say of course, another possibility: Divine Intervention. Though Berry stuck to his worldly explanation, other non-conforming preachers sermonised that God, in his mercy, had locked the jaws of death on behalf of Lee. But considering that Lee (who had served a sentence for theft) was undoubtedly guilty of the extremely brutal murder of an especially God-fearing old lady, it is hard to comprehend why He should have chosen to interfere, apparently uniquely, in this case. The 'hand of God' theory seems less credible than a 'hand of Satan' one.

The Home Secretary, deciding that it would be unfair on Lee to put him through further attempts to hang him, granted a reprieve. In his case, 'imprisonment for life' amounted to twenty-three years. Following his release in December 1907, he did quite well from 'The Man They Could Not Hang' stories in newspapers, the longest of which was turned into a paperback.[1]

Berry was only forty when he resigned in March 1892. He stated that his decision was solely 'on account of Dr Barr interfering with my responsible duty at Kirkdale Gaol, Liverpool, on my last execution there' (of a man named John Conway, who had been almost decapitated). As that unfortunate incident had occurred nearly seven months before, either Berry was in the throes of a delayed psychological reaction or he used the incident as an excuse for resigning. The latter possibility is strengthened by two facts: shortly after becoming an ex-executioner, he became the first such man to publish a book of memoirs[2], and shortly after the book appeared, he embarked upon a long lecture-tour, for which he was very well paid. Though there was nothing in his book that suggested that he disapproved of capital punishment, his lecture was a

1. There is a recording (Island: ILPS 9176) of an almost musical version of the Lee legend, mostly composed by a pop-group called Fairport Convention, who are entirely responsible for singing and playing it.

2. *My Experiences as an Executioner* (Percy Lund & Co, Bradford and London, n.d.; facsimile edition [edited and introduced by Jonathan Goodman], David & Charles, Newton Abbot, and Gale Research, Detroit, 1972.)

mixture of the 'Exciting Episodes' promised on the billboards, and passages of abolitionist propaganda. I noted in the introduction to the facsimile edition of the book, published in 1972, that 'when the lecture engagements petered out, Berry turned his hand to various jobs: as well as being an innkeeper, he was at another time a cloth salesman at north-country markets, at another a bacon salesman on commission. The last years of his life were devoted to evangelistic and temperance work, and he died at his home in Bradford in October 1913.'

Postscript

Here are five reports of *public* executions (three in London, one in Cork, and one in Columbia, Mississippi) which failed to meet the 'hang by the neck till dead' legal requirement.

From the *Gentleman's Magazine*, London, April 1733:

> Four of the seven malefactors who received sentence of death at the Old Bailey on the 7th were executed at Tyburn on the 27th, *viz*, W. Gordan, James Ward and W. Keys for robbery on the highway and W. Norman for a street robbery. The other three, *viz*, H. Harper and Samuel Elms for street robberies and Elizabeth Austen for robbing her mother, who pleaded her belly and was found pregnant, were ordered to be transported for fourteen years. 'Twas reported that Gordan cut his throat just before he was carried out of Newgate for execution and a surgeon sewed it up, but in the *Daily Advertiser* we have the following strange account:
>
> Mr Chovet, a surgeon, having by frequent experiments on dogs discovered that opening the windpipe would prevent the fatal consequences of the halter, undertook Mr Gordan and made an incision in his windpipe, the effect of which was that when Gordan stopped his mouth, nostrils and ears for some time, air enough came through the cavity to continue life. When he was hanged, he was perceived to be alive

after all the rest were dead, and when he had hung three-quarters of an hour, being carried to a house in Tyburn road, he opened his mouth several times and groaned, and, a vein being opened, he bled freely but shortly died.

'Twas thought that if he had been cut down five minutes sooner, he might have recovered.

From the *Gentleman's Magazine*, July 1736:

The grand jury for the county of Middlesex found a bill of indictment against James Bayley and Thomas Reynolds under the Black Act for going armed and disguised and cutting down Ledbury Turnpike. On 9 April 1736, William Bithell and William Morgan were tried for the same offence and hanged. During the trial their fellow turnpike levellers turned up and became so tumultuous that soldiers were called out to preserve order.

Reynolds, a turnpike leveller, condemned with Bayley on 10 April, under the act against going armed and disguised, was hanged at Tyburn on 26 July. He was cut down by the executioner as usual, but as the coffin was being fastened, he thrust back the lid, upon which the executioner would have tied him up again, but the mob prevented it and carried him to a house. There he vomited three pints of blood, but when given a glass of wine he died. Bayley was reprieved.

From the *London Magazine*, November 1740:

Five malefactors were executed at Tyburn on 24 November, *viz*, Thomas Clark, William Meers, Margery Stanton, Eleanor Mumpman for several burglaries and felonies, and William Duell for ravishing, robbing and murdering Sarah Griffin at Acton. The body of Duell was brought to Surgeons Hall to be anatomised, but after it was stripped and laid on the board and one of the servants was washing him in order to be cut, he perceived life in him and found his breath to come quicker and quicker, on which a surgeon took some two ounces of blood from him. In two hours he was able to sit up in his chair and groaned very much and seemed in great agitation but could not speak. He was kept at Surgeons Hall until twelve o'clock at night, the sheriff's officers, who were sent for on this extraordinary occasion, attending. He was then conveyed to Newgate to remain there until he be proved to be the very identical person ordered for execution on the 24th. The next day he was in good health in Newgate, ate his victuals heartily, and asked for his mother. Great numbers of people resorted continually to see him. He did not recollect being hanged but said he had been in a dream.

At the next session at the Old Bailey, he was ordered transported for life.

From the *Gentleman's Magazine*, February 1767:

One Patrick Redmond, having been condemned at Cork in Ireland to be hanged for a street robbery, he was accordingly executed on 24 February, and hung upwards of twenty-eight minutes, when the mob carried off the body to a place appointed, where he was, after five or six hours, actually recovered by a surgeon who made an incision in his windpipe called bronchotomy, which produced the desired effect. The poor fellow has since received his pardon and a genteel collection has been made for him.

The next account – of incidents in Columbia, Mississippi,[1] on 7 February 1894 – needs an introduction, and that is well provided by August Mencken in his book

1. There seems to be uncertainty concerning the date of the last official public hanging in Mississippi. Though the hanging of Clyde Harveston, at Westville, in 1902, was not the last, it warrants being mentioned in this book because of a perhaps supernatural adjunct to it. Apparently, Harveston was found guilty of the murder of a merchant, Frank Ammons, solely because an erstwhile friend, Frank Beavers, implicated him when confessing to the crime; Beavers died naturally a few days after the trial. Harveston protested his innocence till the end, and went so far as to shout, as the noose was tightened: 'God will give you a sign that I am telling the truth!' Though the day is said to have been cloudless, rain started pelting down during the

The Supernatural Murders

By the Neck:[1] 'Some years after the original Ku Klux Klan went out of existence, a similar organisation called the White Caps was formed in the remoter parts of the South for the purpose of terrorising the Negroes. Its members rode round the country at night dressed in white sheets smeared with red paint to simulate blood, but for the most part they confined themselves to threats and resorted to violence only in what they considered extreme cases. Early in 1893, a Negro servant of Will Buckley, a member of the organisation, was selected for such treatment, and, in the absence of Buckley and without his knowledge, one of the bands seized the man and gave him a flogging. Buckley was enraged at this affront to his dignity, and for revenge decided to present the whole matter to the Grand Jury. As a result of his disclosures, three members of the gang were indicted. After completing his testimony, Buckley started for home accompanied by his brother Jim and the Negro, all mounted. When they came to a ford in a small stream,

---

brief period between Harveston's prophesy and his fall. Those who believe that the rain was a 'sign' rely upon a photograph of the execution, which shows a number of opened umbrellas above the crowd – but as the photograph also shows Harveston still erect, it may have been taken before his shout . . . and, of course, one is perplexed as to why so many spectators carried umbrellas on a cloudless day.

Perhaps the last public hanging in Mississippi was of Will Mack, a negro, at Brandon, near the state capital of Jackson, on Thursday, 23 July 1909: a sweltering day, according to the *Brandon News*, 'with a thrifty trucker selling large, juicy, red-meated watermelons to those who wished something cooling, and the peanut vendor, the ice cream cone seller and the pop-stand fellow doing a rushing business . . . to a crowd that had no reason to be other than good-humoured about the hanging of a criminal whose death every decent person in the world said should be the penalty of rape. Some ladies were present; many little children, some with parents – and others without, as they were large enough to keep from being mashed in the crowd; there were a few nursing infants who tugged at the mother's breasts while the mother kept her eyes on the gallows – she didn't want to lose any part of the programme she had come miles to see – to tell about to the neighbours at home who were unable to be on hand – to think about while awake; to doubtless see in horrible dreams when asleep, and to never want to see again.' But Will Mack's may not have been Mississippi's 'last necktie party'. That term headlined a letter from an Ernest Ishee that was published in the *Jackson Clarion Leader* of 6 August 1979: '. . . I wish to inform you that the execution of Will Mack at Brandon in 1909 was not the last public hanging in the state. There was one in Bay Springs in 1912 or 1913. My father and two older brothers went to the event.'

1. Hastings House, New York, 1942.

someone concealed in the underbush shot and killed Will Buckley. The other two were fired on also, but escaped. The scene of the killing was near the home of a family called Purvis, and as Will Purvis, one of the sons, was generally believed to be a member of the White Caps, a neighbour who had a grudge against the family had little difficulty arousing the neighbourhood against the boy. Purvis was arrested and lodged in jail. At his trial, he produced witnesses who testified that he was nowhere near the scene at the time of the murder, but Jim Buckley, who had witnessed the killing, was positive in his identification of Purvis as the man who had shot his brother, so Purvis was found guilty by the jury and sentenced to hang.'

From the *New Orleans Item*:

Purvis's hour approaches. The scaffold, firm and portentous, has been erected on the courtyard square; the rope has been secured, the knot tied and examined by a committee. The black cap, symbol of death, is ready. The people gather and struggle for points of vantage. The minister is praying and consoling the boy the best he can. The death march begins.

With face bleached by confinement within prison walls, but with a firm step and steady eye, young Purvis ascends the scaffold. As he looks over that closely packed and vacuously yawping throng, the young man sees few friendly faces. Feeling against him has been intense and most people believe he is about to expiate a crime for which he should pay the extreme penalty. Everyone is waiting for one thing before the final drop. It is the confession of the boy that he did commit murder. But Purvis speaks simply these plain words which amaze them:

'You are taking the life of an innocent man. There are people here who know who did commit the crime, and if they will come forward and confess, I will go free.'

As Purvis finishes his simple plea, the sheriff and

three deputies adjust the rope about his neck, his feet and arms are pinioned, and the black cap is placed over his face. All is ready, but the meticulous deputy who has tied the hangman's knot sees an ungainly rope's end sticking out. One must be neat at such functions, and he steps up and snips the end flush with the knot. 'Tell me when you are ready,' Purvis remarks, not knowing that the doomed is never given this information lest he brace himself.

Nothing is heard save the persistent and importunate prayer of the minister. The executioner takes the hatchet. As he draws it back to sever the stay rope holding the trap on which Purvis stands, strong men tremble and a woman screams and faints. The blow descends, the trap falls, and the body of Will Purvis darts like a plummet towards the sharp jerk of a sudden death.

Terror and awe gripped the throng as Purvis fell towards his death. Those few men who had watched others hang averted their faces. Others who had never witnessed a like event, and who could not appreciate the morbid horror of it, stared open-mouthed. But those who looked did not see the boy dangle and jerk and become motionless in death. The rope failed to perform the service ordained for it by law. Instead of tightening like a garroter's bony fingers on the neck of the youth, the hangman's knot untwisted and Purvis fell to the ground unhurt save for a few abrasions on his skin caused by the slipping of the rope.

No tongue can describe and no pen can indite the feeling of horror that seized and held the vast throng. For a moment the watchers remained motionless; then, moved by an impelling wonder, they crowded forward, crushing one another with the force of their movement. In a moment the silence broke. Excited murmurs began to emanate from the crowd. 'What's the matter? Did the noose slip?' someone asked. Others wondered if there had been some trick in tying the knot. But those charged with the duty of making it fast said there was not, and their statement was verified by a committee that had examined the rope and the knot just before its adjustment around the man's neck.

Besides, there could hardly have been a desire on the part of any of the officials to save Purvis. The organisation with which he was supposed to have been connected had given them too much trouble and his trial and conviction had cost the county too much money to warrant the belief that any means would have been used at that late hour to circumvent the execution of the death sentence.

Somewhat dazed, Purvis staggered to his feet. The black cap slipped from his face and the large blue eyes of the boy blinked in the sunlight. Most of the crowd stood dumbfounded and the officials were aghast. Purvis realised the situation sooner than any of them and, turning to the sheriff, said, 'Let's have it over with.' At the same time the boy, bound hand and feet as he was, began to hop towards the steps of the scaffold and had mounted the first step before the silence was broken.

An uneasy tremor swept the crowd. The slight cleavage in opinion which before had been manifest concerning the boy's guilt or innocence now seemed to widen into a real division. Many of those who had been most urgent that Purvis be hanged began to feel within themselves the first flutter of misgiving. This feeling might never have been crystallised into words had it not been for a simple little incident. One of the officials on the platform had reached for the rope but found it was just beyond his fingers' ends. Stooping, he called out to Dr Ford, who was standing beneath, 'Toss that rope up here, will you, Doctor?' Dr Ford started mechanically to obey. He picked up the rope and looked at it. The crowd watched him intently. Here was a man who had been most bitter against the White Caps, a man who knew that Purvis had been a member of that notorious body, and yet everyone knew that he was one of the few who refused to believe the boy was guilty. Throwing the rope down, he said, 'I won't do any such damn thing. That boy's been hung once too many times now.'

Electrically, the crowd broke its silence. Cries of 'Don't let him hang!' were heard clashing with 'Hang him! He's guilty!' A few of Purvis's friends and relatives were galvanised into action. They pushed their way forward, ready to act, but the greater proportion of the spectators were still morbidly curious to see the death struggles of the boy. Some of them really believed the ends of justice were about to be thwarted and tensed themselves to prevent any attempt to free him.

At this moment the Reverend J. Sibley, whose sympathy and prayer had helped to sustain the mother during her trying ordeal, sprang up the steps of the scaffold ahead of the stumbling boy. He was a preacher of the most eloquent type and of fine physique and commanding appearance. His eyes flashed with the fire of a great inspiration as he raised his hands and stood motionless until the eyes of the spectators became centered upon him. 'All who want to see this boy hanged a second time,' he shouted, 'hold up their hands.'

The crowd remained transfixed. There is a difference between the half-shamed desire of a man to stand in a large throng and watch his neighbour die and the willingness of that man to stand before others and signify by raising his hand that he insists upon the other's extinction. Not a hand went up. 'All who are opposed to hanging Will Purvis a second time,' cried the Reverend Sibley, 'hold up your hands.' Every hand in the crowd went up as if magically raised by a universal lever.

Pandemonium ensued. Men tore their hair and threw their hats into the air, swearing that this man should not be hanged again. Public sentiment had changed in an instant. Before the hanging, they thought him a vile and contemptible murderer; now they believed him spotless as an angel. But even while the mob was joyously acclaiming Purvis as one returned from the shadow of death, and men and women were surging forward to congratulate him on his miraculous escape, the menace of the law still hung over him, reluctant to allow him to escape.

The sheriff and his deputies were undoubtedly in an awkward position. They had been commissioned to carry out the sentence of the court and they were bound by their oaths of office to do so. Should they flout the authority of the court merely because a number of emotional spectators had decided out of hand not to allow the defendant to be hanged, they would be liable to impeachment and imprisonment. On the other hand, to attempt to hang Purvis the second time in the face of 5000 healthy spectators, nearly every one determined to prevent such action, would be suicidal.

It was clearly an unusual situation and one which called for the finely balanced judgment of a legally trained mind. The sheriff turned to Dr Ford and said, 'These folks do not want to see Purvis hanged again, Doctor, but I am bound in honour to carry out the sentence of the court. Because the rope slipped I can't see that the situation is altered. What do you think?'

Dr Ford suggested that a judge or lawyer be sought. The sheriff called for a judge, but none was in the crowd. Then he asked for lawyers, and for a moment it seemed that the lawyers had also decided not to attend the execution; but finally a young attorney answered the summons. After considering the matter in its various apsects, he reluctantly informed the sheriff that it was his belief that Purvis must be 'hanged by the neck until dead', according to the meaning of the sentence. The sheriff as reluctantly agreed.

Meanwhile, activity had been resumed upon the scaffold by the executioners. The crowd had quieted and waited to hear the results of the conference, which took place near the scaffold. The sheriff looked at the throng. Its temper was probably heated, so that an attempt to hang Purvis again might result in additional tragedy, yet he did not see how he could avoid making the attempt at least. Dr Ford, who had listened with chagrin to the attorney's opinion, finally spoke up with determination. 'I don't agree with you.

Now, if I go upon that scaffold and ask three hundred men to stand by me and prevent the hanging, what are you going to do about it?'

Both the sheriff and the attorney were taken aback at this suggestion. They realised that they would be powerless in the face of such action. 'I'm ready to do it too,' added Dr Ford. Suddenly the sheriff turned, walked to Purvis, and as the crowd cheered, began to loosen the bonds of the prisoner. Dr Ford, fearing he would release Purvis, interfered. 'Don't let him go,' he said. 'Take him back to his cell.' Dr Ford was afraid that if Purvis was released, the White Caps would assume a more important place in the minds of several citizens than the courts, that the murder of Buckley would be condoned, and the possibility of capturing the real murderer made more remote than with Purvis in prison to await further legal action. It was with difficulty that Purvis was carried back to jail, so persistent was the crowd in its demand for his freedom.

Henry Banks, one of the staff of executioners, afterwards gave his version of why the knot had slipped. 'The rope was too thick in the first place,' he said. 'It was made of new grass and was very springy. After the first man tied the noose, he let the free end hang out. It was this way when the tests were made, but when it came to placing this knot around Purvis's neck, it looked untidy. The hangman didn't want to be accredited with this kind of a job, so he cut the rope flush with the noose-knot. It looked neat, but when the weight of Purvis's body was thrown against it, the rope slipped and the knot became untied.'

August Mencken: 'After the fiasco at the scaffold, Purvis was returned to his cell and a legal battle was started to free him. His case was based on Article V of the Constitution of the United States, prohibiting double jeopardy, but the Mississippi Supreme Court decided against him and he was re-sentenced to hang. While he was awaiting execution the second time, his friends broke into the jail and carried him to a hiding-place on a remote farm. Two years afterwards,

Jim Buckley changed his mind and announced that he was not sure that Purvis was the man, and in consequence the Governor commuted Purvis's sentence to life imprisonment. The fugitive then returned from the farm and started serving his sentence, and on 19 December 1898 he received a full pardon. Nineteen years afterwards, one Joe Beard was gathered in by the Holy Rollers, and, in ridding himself of his sins, confessed, among other things, that he and one Louis Thornhill were the men who killed Buckley. The Legislature of Mississippi thereupon voted Purvis $5000 as compensation for the time he spent in jail.'

Defending the 'Witch-Burners'

EDMUND PEARSON

THERE WILL BE WRITTEN some day, it is to be hoped, a tragic drama upon one of the most terrible and mysterious events in American history: the witchcraft trials at Salem. Longfellow wrote a play in verse around them, while other authors have compiled histories or written poems. The subject still awaits adequate treatment in dramatic form.[1]

Today, the witch-hunters of 1692 have only two functions. They afford a topic for jokes and playful allusions, as a kind of grotesque Hallowe'en party; or else they are used as a convenient stick with which to belabour the New England Puritans.

If a Broadway producer gets into conflict with the police because, in his vocabulary, nudity is synonymous with Art, and smut with Sophistication, he usually founds his defence

---

1. EDITOR'S NOTE. This essay was first published, in the US *Vanity Fair*, in April 1931. The subject received adequate treatment in dramatic form in *The Crucible* by Arthur Miller (himself a victim of Senator Joseph McCarthy's hunt for Communist 'Witches'), which was first produced on Broadway in 1953, winning the Antoinette Perry ('Tony') Award. The play was produced at the Liverpool Playhouse in 1957 (while I was stage director there), with a cast including, in order of appearance, Terence Knapp (now Professor of Drama and Theatre at the University of Hawaii), Thelma Barlow, Robert James, Mona Bruce (now Mrs Robert James), Richard Briers, Ann Davies (now Mrs Richard Briers), and Helen Lindsay (now the wife of Alan Pikford, who designed the settings). The French movie, *Les Sorcières de Salem* (1957), starring Simone Signoret, Yves Montand and Mylène Demongeot, was based on the play. Twenty years before, a Hollywood movie, *Maid of Salem*, reminiscent of the events in Massachusetts, starred Claudette Colbert, Fred MacMurray and Bonita Granville.

upon a reference to the 'Salem witch-burners'. If a publisher brings out a notorious and usually unimportant book — hoping and praying with all his heart that the Watch-and-Ward will give him the advertisement of an attempt at suppression — he is sure to be heard muttering something about 'Salem witch-burners'.

From folk whose information about history is so dim as to be non-existent, nothing else is expected. But a considerable number of writers who are careful to inform us that they are among the liberals or the intellectuals have two pet weapons: the clubs they throw at old Queen Victoria, and the stones they hurl at Salem. When some patient and hopeful correspondent writes in to the papers, to inform these people, for the four-hundredth time, that the Salem witches were *not* burned, the information is treated with that contempt for historical accuracy which is the hallmark of this type of intellectual.

The liberality and tolerance of these liberals always end when they look over into the borders of New England. They are prepared to believe that some Boston policeman who is making an ass of himself (and who is named O'Halloran or Ivanowski or Repetti) is a lineal descendant of Cotton Mather or the Rev Nicholas Noyes and is all ready to drag a lot of old ladies off to a bonfire in the backyard of the House of the Seven Gables.

The playwright who is content to accept the tremendous dramatic possibilities of the witchcraft trials will have his incidents at hand. He cannot improve upon them. But he must indicate the atmosphere of the time. He must let his audience understand that this belief in the reality of Satan, and in the foul betrayal of Christ implied in the sale of a human soul, was not a sudden invention of the colonists, but something brought with them from England. He must show the people of Massachusetts as living on the edge of a wilderness which was inhabited by savages, who frequently descended upon the lonely settlements, and scalped women and children. And he must make it plain that the colonists were people who were accustomed to regard the salvation of their souls as at least as important as the safety of their bodies.

Today, this is reversed. We, or many of us, never worry about our souls at all, but give the most painful and minute care to the welfare of our bodies – make this, in fact, a religion. And here, perhaps, is the best parallel between our mental condition and that of our ancestors. Suppose, for the sake of argument, that two or three hundred years from now the germ theory of disease should be entirely discredited. With what scornful derision the folk of that time would look back upon us – upon our vaccinations and inoculations, upon our elaborate and expensive sanitation, upon the punishments and social ostracism visited upon those who break sanitary laws. How they would jeer at the hysteric fears expressed when false rumours went about in 1898 that 'Spanish agents' were infecting the water-supplies of cities with disease germs!

Well, just as science has proved to our satisfaction the possibility of contracting disease from bacteria, so the science of their day had proved to the men of 1692 that a human being could make a contract with the Devil, and acquire the power to torment and afflict innocent persons. The Bible commands the execution of witches; the laws of all Christian countries provided for it; belief in its necessity was not the invention of New England Puritans, but was shared by all sects, by Catholic and Protestant alike. The great text-book of witch-finders, *Malleus Maleficarum*, was written by two German priests, at the command of the Pope.

The drama about the outbreak of persecution in America should begin, I think, on one of those dark winter nights, around the fire in the kitchen of the Rev Mr Parris. Here are gathered ten or a dozen girls, one of them only nine years old, some of them twenty; most of them adolescent trouble-makers and neurotics. The little twelve-year-old hell cat, Ann Putnam, was one of the few who could write her own name. They are learning palmistry, necromancy, magic and spiritism from Mr Parris's West Indian negro-woman, Tituba. Things have gone so far, under Tituba's stories of *obi*, of witches and wizards, that the girls begin to see ghosts in the dark corners; begin to go into fits, to writhe on the floor and imitate animals. The hysteria is contagious, frightful, and it is the local doctor who says that these children are bewitched.

There can be little doubt that some of these victims lost control of themselves, and were not acting a part. Their contortions, later in the Courtroom, their distorted bodies and rolling eyes, their lips bitten until they bled, were not the result of acting, but were genuine and frightful. Some of them may have realised what they were doing, and were deliberately malicious, or fond of notoriety and power. Some must have been under the influence of older and more crafty persons, because when the accusations began, there was many an instance of the deliberate satisfaction of an ancient grudge. Salem Village, like every other community, had its share of harmless folk, its share of the noble and courageous, and its share of the spiteful or even murderous.

For one of the trials, to show on the stage, the playwright might select that of George Jacobs. This tall, old man, bent and leaning on two canes, had offended the Putnam family in a law-suit. He knew the enmity he faced; and the peril in which he stood. He looked with amazement and horror at the girls, convulsed on the floor: objects of pity and terror to all in Court. He knew he had no part in their agony. Yet they pointed at him and screamed that he was tormenting them. It was the belief that if a witch could be made to touch his victim, the 'witch fluid' went back into his body, and the victim was relieved. Jacobs was put through this farcical ceremony, and the girls became calm. All the judges were convinced, and the crowd, inside and out-doors, demanded a verdict against the prisoner.

Imagine a Court of today, into which had been brought four or five children dying of typhoid fever. Suppose that witnesses testified that the prisoner, an old man, had been detected in putting the germs of this disease into the children's milk. The wrath and detestation felt by the spectators would be something like that of the people in the Salem Court when Jacobs was on trial.

In some of his remarks he comes down to us as one of the first of the Yankees: a man of grim humour, disgusted by all this nonsense, even if he could not understand it.

'Here are them that accuse you of witchcraft,' said a judge.

'Well,' replied Jacobs, 'let us hear who they are, and what they are.'

Later, he laughed when one of the shrieking girls was produced, and asked the Court if they could believe this to be true.

'You tax me for a wizard,' said he, 'you may as well tax me for a buzzard.' But his contempt did him no good; the delusion did not pass soon enough to save him, and he was carried off to execution. He, and three or four other men, and a number of women, most of them old, and some of them crazed, were carted up to Gallows Hill. Executions took place on two or three different occasions in that dreadful summer. Some of the victims spoke up with spirit. Old Sarah Good, being told by the Rev Mr Noyes that she was a witch and she knew she was a witch, retorted:

'*You* are a liar. I am no more a witch than you are a wizard, and if you take away my life, God will give you blood to drink.' The legend is that Mr Noyes died from a 'stroke' which caused a rush of blood into his throat. This incident was afterwards effectively used by Nathaniel Hawthorne.

The Rev Mr Burroughs, who had been dragged back from Maine to be convicted and executed, stood upon the scaffold and repeated the Lord's prayer with such solemnity that many in the crowd murmured against the officers of the law. But this did not trouble the Rev Mr Noyes (an active agent of the Devil, if one was present at all), who merely pointed at the bodies dangling from the beam and remarked:

'How sad to see eight firebrands of Hell hanging there!'

An English author and exceedingly high-churchman, Dr Montague Summers, devoutly believes in witchcraft, and is convinced that a 'coven' of witches did exist in New England, and that the execution of the Rev Mr Burroughs, and of two or three others out of the nineteen, was therefore just. Professor George Kittredge, a New Englander, who does not believe in the reality of witchcraft, puts it somewhat more rationally:

'Many persons who have been executed for witchcraft have supposed themselves to be guilty, and have actually been guilty in intent.'

There were many *confessions* in Salem. Fifty-five are recorded. These came from people who had been trying some kind of black magic, or from those who noticed that if one confessed he escaped the gallows. The sufferers were, therefore, men and women who would not perjure themselves to save their necks.

Professor Kittredge further points out that witchcraft, in one form or another, is *still* believed in by a majority of the human race; that trials and one death sentence took place in England after the end of the Salem delusion, and that executions occurred in Europe for another hundred years; that the total number of persons executed in New England is inconsiderable in view of what went on in Europe; and that the public repentance of judge and jury in Massachusetts has no parallel in history.

If we look upon what happened in one corner of America, a few centuries ago, as an incident in the general history of us all, then we all share in its shame and disgrace. But if we practise the provincial custom of making attacks upon some one state or region, we must look to our own glass-houses. We cannot afford to say much about the Salem witches if we chance to live where the custom of lynching negroes, often innocent negroes, is extenuated today. Nor can we, in New York, say much about Salem after we have considered the 'negro plot' of 1741, fifty years after the end of the witchcraft trials. In an hysterical panic, eighteen negroes and four white men were hanged, fifty negroes were sent into slavery, and fourteen negroes were burned at the stake in the city of New York. When an editorial writer or columnist next prepares some stinging allusion to 'Salem witch-burners', I recommend these events to his notice.

Postscript

The following account of one of the trials is from *The Wonders of The Invisible World* by the Rev Cotton Mather, the most famous or infamous of all the New England Puritans, who is said to have 'combined a mystical strain (he believed in witchcraft) with a modern scientific interest (he supported smallpox inoculation)'. In May 1692, when fifty accused witches were in various jails awaiting trial, his father, Increase Mather, who was also a Congregational minister, persuaded the newly-arrived Royal Governor of Massachusetts to appoint twelve ministers to set up guidelines for the conduct of the trials. According to Leo Bonfanti, author of a pamphlet, *The Witchcraft Hysteria,*[1] 'The appointed ministers, convinced that the Devil had the power to assume the shape of anyone he chose to impersonate, recommended, among other things, that spectral evidence – instances in which the spectre of a person was seen performing acts of witchcraft while the person was elsewhere and unaware of what was taking place – should not be permitted. Once they had completed their task, they assigned Cotton Mather the responsibility of writing the final draft. Although he followed their recommendations faithfully, he nullified the one pertaining to spectral evidence by adding his praise for the authorities and the members of the Court for their diligence in detecting and prosecuting the witches to this date. He urged them to continue their good work, being careful in doing so that they were always guided by the laws of God and the English statutes.'

1. Pride Publications, Wakefield, Mass., n.d.

The Trial of Susanna Martin
at the Court of Oyer and Terminer,
Held by Adjournment at Salem, 29 June 1692[1]

Susanna Martin, pleading *Not Guilty* to the Indictment of *Witchcraft* brought in against her, there were produced the Evidences of many Persons very sensibly and grievously Bewitched, who all complained of the Prisoner at the Bar as the Person whom they believed the cause of their Miseries. And now, as well as in the other Trials, there was an extraordinary Endeavour by *Witchcrafts*, with Cruel and frequent Fits, to hinder the poor Sufferers from giving in their Complaints, which the Court was forced with much Patience to obtain, by much waiting and watching for it.

An account was given of what passed at her first Examination before the Magistrates. As to the Cast of her *Eye*, which struck the afflicted People to the Ground, whether they saw that Cast or no, there were these among other Passages between the Magistrates and the Examinate:

Magistrate	Pray, what ails these People?
Martin	I don't know.
Magistrate	But what do you think ails them?
Martin	I don't desire to spend my Judgment upon it.
Magistrate	Don't you think they are bewitched?
Martin	No, I do not think they are.
Magistrate	Tell us your Thoughts about them, then.
Martin	No, my thoughts are my own when they are in, but when they are out they are another's. Their Master —
Magistrate	Their Master? Who do you think is their Master?
Martin	If they be dealing in the Black Art, you may know as well as I.
Magistrate	Well, what have you done towards this?
Martin	Nothing at all.

1. EDITOR'S NOTE. I have made slight changes, mainly of spelling and punctuation, to Cotton Mather's account.

Magistrate	Why, 'tis you or your Appearance.
Martin	I cannot help it.
Magistrate	Is it not *your* Master? How comes your Appearance to hurt these?
Martin	How do I know? He that appeared in the Shape of *Samuel*, a glorified Saint, may appear in anyone's Shape.

It was then also noted in her, as in others like her, that if the Afflicted went to approach her, they were flung down to the Ground. And, when she was asked the reason of it, she said, *I cannot tell; it may be that the Devil bears me more Malice than another.*

The Court, alarumed by these Things, inquired further into the Conversation of the Prisoner, to see what might occur to render the Accusations further credible. Whereupon, *John Allen* of *Salisbury,* testified that he refused, because of the weakness of his Oxen, to Cart some Staves at the request of this *Martin*, and she was displeased at it and said, *His Oxen should never do him much more Service.* Whereupon, this Deponent said, *Dost thou threaten me, thou old Witch? I'll throw thee into the Brook*: Which to avoid, she flew over the Bridge and escaped. But as he was going home, one of his Oxen tired, so that he was forced to Unyoke him. He then put his Oxen, with many more, upon *Salisbury Beach*, where Cattle did use to get food. In a few days, all the Oxen upon the Beach were found, by their Tracks, to have run unto the Mouth of *Merrimack-River*; the next day they were found come ashore upon *Plum-Island*. They that sought them used all imaginable gentleness, but they would still run away with a violence that seemed wholly Diabolical till they came near the mouth of *Merrimack-River*, when they ran right into the Sea, swimming as far as they could be seen. One of them then swam back again, with a swiftness amazing to the Beholders who stood ready to receive him and help up his tired Carcass: but the Beast ran furiously up into the Island, and thence through the Marshes, up into *Newbury* Town, and so up into the Woods; after a while he was found near

Amesbury. Of fourteen good Oxen, there was only this one saved: The rest were cast up, some in one place and some in another, all Drowned.

John Atkinson testified that he exchanged a Cow with a Son of *Susanna Martin's,* whereat she muttered and was unwilling he should have it. Going to receive this Cow, tho he Hamstring'd her and Halter'd her, she, once a Tame Creature, grew so mad that they could scarce get her along. She broke all the Ropes that were fastened unto her, and though she were tied fast unto a Tree, yet she made her escape and gave them such further trouble as they could ascribe to no cause but Witchcraft.

Bernard Peache testified that, being in Bed on the Lord's-day Night, he heard a scrabbling at the Window, whereat he then saw *Susanna Martin* come in and jump down upon the Floor. She took hold of his Feet and, drawing his Body up into a Heap, lay upon him near Two Hours, in all which time he could neither speak nor stir. At length, when he could begin to move, he laid hold of her Hand, and pulling it up to his Mouth, bit three of her Fingers, as he judged, unto the Bone. Whereupon she went from the Chamber, down the Stairs, and out at the Door. This Deponent thereupon called unto the People of the House, to advise them of what passed, and did follow her. The People saw her not; but there was a Bucket at the Left-hand of the Door, and a drop of Blood was found upon it; several more drops of Blood were upon the Snow newly fallen abroad: there was the print of her two Feet just without the Threshold, but no more sign of any Footing further off.

At another time this Deponent was desired by the Prisoner to come unto a Husking of Corn at her House; and she said, *If he did not come, it were better that he did!* He went not, but the Night following, *Susanna Martin,* as he judged, and another came towards him. One of them said, *Here he is!* but he, having a Quarter-staff, made a Blow at them. The Roof of the Barn broke his Blow, but following them to the Window, he made another Blow at them and struck them down; yet they got up and got out, and he saw no more of them. About this time, there was a Rumour about the Town that *Susanna Martin* had a Broken Head, but the Deponent could say nothing to that.

Robert Downer testified that, this Prisoner being some Years ago prosecuted at Court for being a Witch, he then said unto her, *He believed she was a Witch.* Whereat she, being dissatisfied, said *That some She-Devil would shortly fetch him away!* Which words were heard by others as well as himself. The Night following as he lay in his Bed, there came in at the Window the likeness of a *Cat*, which flew upon him, took fast hold of his Throat, lay on him a considerable while, and almost killed him. At length he remembered what *Susanna Martin* had threatened the Day before; and with much striving he cried out, *Avoid, thou She-Devil! In the Name of God the Father, The Son, and the Holy Ghost, Avoid!* Whereupon it left him, leaped on the Floor, and flew out at the Window.

And there also came in several Testimonies that before ever *Downer* spoke a word of this Accident, *Susanna Martin* and her Family had related *How this* Downer *had been handled!*

John Kembal testified that *Susanna Martin*, upon a Causeless Disgust, had threatened him about a certain Cow of his, *That she should never do him any more Good:* and it came to pass accordingly, for soon after the Cow was found stark dead on the dry Ground, without any Distemper to be discerned upon her. He was followed with a strange Death upon more of his Cattle, whereof he lost in one Spring to the value of Thirty Pounds.

The said *John Kembal* had a further Testimony to give in against the Prisoner which was truly admirable:

Being desirous to furnish himself with a Dog, he applied himself to buy one of this *Martin*, who had a Bitch with Whelps in her House. But as she would not let him have his choice, he said he would supply himself at one *Blezdels*. Having marked a Puppy which he liked at *Blezdels*, he met *George Martin*, the Husband of the Prisoner, who asked him, *Whether he would not have one of his Wife's Puppies?*

and he answered, *No*. The same Day, one *Edmund Eliot*, being at *Martin's* House, heard *George Martin* relate where this *Kembal* had been and what he had said. Whereupon *Susanna Martin* replied, *If I live, I'll give him Puppies enough!* A few days after, when this *Kembal* was coming out of the Woods, there arose a little Black Cloud in the N.W. and *Kembal* immediately felt a force upon him which made him not able to avoid running upon the stumps of Trees, albeit he had a broad, plain Cart-way before him; tho' he had his Axe on his Shoulder to endanger him in his Falls, he could not forbear going out of his way to tumble over them. When he came below the Meeting House, there appeared unto him a little thing like a *Puppy*, of a Darkish Colour; it shot backwards and forwards between his Legs. He had the Courage to use all possible Endeavours of Cutting it with his Axe, but he could not Hit it: the Puppy gave a jump from him and went, as to him it seemed, into the Ground. Going a little further, there appeared unto him another Puppy, somewhat bigger than the first but as Black as a Coal. Its Motions were quicker than those of his Axe; it flew at his Belly and away; then at his Throat; over his Shoulder one way and then over his Shoulder another way. His Heart now began to fail him and he thought the Dog would have torn his Throat out. But he recovered himself and called upon God in his Distress; and naming the Name of JESUS CHRIST, it vanished away at once. The Deponent spoke not one Word of these Accidents, for fear of affrighting his Wife. But the next Morning, when *Edmund Eliot* went into *Martin's* House, this Woman asked him where *Kembal* was? He replied, *At home abed, for ought he knew*. She said, *They say he was frighted last Night*. *Eliot* asked, *With what?* She answered, *With Puppies*. *Eliot* asked *Where she heard of it, for he had heard nothing of it*. She rejoined, *About the Town*. *Kembal* had mentioned the Matter to no Creature living.

William Brown testified that, Heaven having blessed him with a most Pious and Prudent Wife, this Wife of his one day met with *Susanna Martin*; but when she approached just unto her, *Martin* vanished out of sight and left her extremely affrighted. After which time, *Martin* often appeared unto her, giving her no little trouble; and when she came, his Wife was visited with Birds that sorely pecked and pricked her; and sometimes, a Bunch, like a Pullet's Egg, would rise in her Throat, ready to choke her, till she cried out, *Witch, you shan't choke me!* While this good Woman was in this extremity, the Church appointed a Day of Prayer on her behalf; whereupon her Trouble ceased; she saw not *Martin* as formerly; and the Church gave Thanks for her Deliverance. But a considerable while after, she being Summoned to give some Evidence at the Court against this *Martin*, *Martin* came behind her while she was milking her Cow and said unto her, *For thy defaming me at Court, I'll make thee the miserablest Creature in the World.* Soon after, she fell into a strange kind of distemper and became horribly frantic and uncapable of any reasonable Action; the Physicians declared that her Distemper was preternatural and that some Devil had certainly betwitched her. And in that condition she now remained.

Sarah Atkinson testified that *Susanna Martin* came from *Amesbury* to her House at *Newbury* in an extraordinary Season, when it was not fit for any to Travel. She came (as she said, unto *Atkinson*) all that long way on Foot. She bragged and she showed how dry she was; nor could it be perceived that so much as the Soles of her Shoes were wet. *Atkinson* was amazed at it, and professed that she should herself have been wet up to the knees if she had come so far; but *Martin* replied, *She scorned to be Drabbled* [made wet and muddy]. It was noted that this Testimony at the Trial cast her in a very singular Confusion.

John Pressy testified that several times one Evening he was unaccountably Bewildered near a Field of *Martin's*, as one under an Enchantment; at length he saw a marvellous Light, about the bigness of a Half-bushel, near two Rod away. He went and struck at it with a Stick, laying on it with all his might. He gave it near forty blows, and felt it a palpable substance. But going from it, his Heels were struck up and he was laid with his Back on the Ground, sliding, as he thought, into a Pit, whence he recover'd by taking hold on a Bush; afterwards he could find no such Pit in the place. Having, after his Recovery, gone five or six Rod, he saw *Susanna Martin* standing on his Left-hand, as the Light had done before, but they changed no words with one another. He could scarce find his House on his Return; but at length he got home extremely affrighted. The next day, it was upon Inquiry understood that *Martin* was in a miserable condition with pains and hurts that were upon her.

It was further testified by this Deponent that twenty years ago, after he had given some Evidence against *Susanna Martin*, she gave him foul words about it; she said, *He should never prosper more;* particularly, *That he should never have more than two Cows; that tho' he was likely to have more, yet he should never have them.* And from that very day to this, he could never exceed that number; some strange thing or other still prevented his having any more.

Jervis Ring testified that about seven years ago he was oftentimes and grievously oppressed in the Night, but saw not who troubled him, until at last he, Lying perfectly Awake, plainly saw *Susanna Martin* approach him. She came to him and forcibly bit him by the Finger, so that the Print of the bite is now, so long after, to be seen upon him.

Besides all of these Evidences, there was a most wonderful Account by one *Joseph Ring*, who has been strangely carried about by *Demons* from one *Witch-meeting* to another for near two years together; for one quarter of this time, they made him Dumb, tho' he is now again able to speak.

Afterwards, this poor Man would be visited with unknown shapes which would force him away with them unto unknown Places, where he saw Meetings, Feastings and Dancings; and after his return, having been hurried along through the Air, he gave Demonstrations to the Neighbours that he had indeed been so transported. When he was brought unto these hellish Meetings, one of the first Things they did to him was to give him a knock on the Back, whereupon he was ever as if bound with Chains, uncapable of stirring out of the place till they should release him. He related that there often came to him a Man who presented him a *Book* whereto he would have him set his Hand, promising to him that he should then have whatever he desired, and presenting him with all the delectable Things, Persons and Places that he could imagine. But as he refused to subscribe, the business would end with dreadful Shapes, Noises and Screeches, which almost scared him out of his Wits. Once with the Book, there was a Pen offered him, and an Ink-horn with Liquor in it that seemed like Blood: But he never touched it.

This Man, *Joseph Ring*, did now affirm that he saw the Prisoner at several of these hellish Rendezvouzes.

Note that this Woman was one of the most impudent, scurrilous, wicked Creatures in the World — and she did throughout her whole Trial expose herself to be such a one.

Yet when she was asked what she had to say for herself, her chief Plea was:

She had led a most virtuous and holy Life.

EDITOR'S NOTE. Just over a fortnight before Susanna Martin was tried, the first of the persons convicted of witchcraft had been hanged. Susanna was one of five who were hanged on 19 July 1692. There were five more executions on 19 August. On 19 September a man was pressed to death for refusing to answer the charges against him. Three days later, his wife was one of the last eight persons hanged.

In the following May, the Royal Governor of Massachusetts, having received instructions from England, pardoned everyone who had been found Guilty or who was in jail awaiting trial (pardons for the untried!), and those who had made confessions so as to save their lives, and granted amnesty to those, perhaps as many as a couple of hundred, who had fled from the jurisdiction of the Court.

None of the 'afflicted accusers' or their influential supporters was ever brought to trial. Ann Putnam — who, though she was not quite into her teens in 1692, is generally believed to have been 'the leader of the tormented maidens' — humbled herself at church-services in Salem Village Church. Subsequently becoming a recluse, allegedly broken in mind and health, she lingered on to the age of thirty-six. It is an interesting question, whether she should have been more or less affrighted by the prospect of a rendezvous with Satan than by expectation of an appearance before the Judge of all men.

(So far as I am aware, no journalist, social worker or epidemiologist — or anyone else, for that matter — has thought to compare the Salem hysteria of exactly three centuries ago with or to recent sudden outbreaks in English towns and on Scottish islands of sound-alike accusations by many local children of sexual molestation. Such a comparison might be interesting — and might even be valuable, if it were done by a person who was not sure of answers before he asked questions.)

The Protracted Murder of Gregory Rasputin

LADY LUCY WINGFIELD

EDITOR'S NOTE. The Russian prince, Felix Yousoupoff (who was also entitled to the title of Count Sumarokov-Elston), was the husband of Princess Irina, daughter of the Grand Duke Alexander Mikhailovich and Tsar Nicholas II's sister, the Grand Duchess Xenia. In 1916, when he was twenty-nine, he, with others, murdered the 'Satanic Monk', Gregory Rasputin (whose full surname was Rasputin-Novy or -Novykh). Rasputin was believed by many (foremost among them, both royal and noble 'Sister-Disciples') to be a miracle-worker, and by comparatively few others to be a dangerous charlatan; the majority of both the adorers and the haters agreed that he was the most influential man in Russia — and more powerful even than the Tsar. Just what Yousoupoff's motive was — whether political, patriotic, sexual or superstitious — is argued over by people who believe that motives for murder are always finite and tidy, capable of being described in one or at most two words. Leon Trotsky, a founder of the Communist Party, considered that the murder of Rasputin 'was carried out in the manner of a scenario designed for people of bad taste'. (In 1940, which was Trotsky's thirteenth year of Stalin-imposed exile from the USSR, he himself was murdered, also untastefully — with an ice-axe wielded by a Stalinist agent who, having pretended admiration for Trotsky, had been welcomed into his heavily guarded villa near Mexico City.)

Lady Lucy Wingfield was the fascinatingly beautiful
wife of the diplomat Sir Charles, who from 1915 until
1919 was attached to the British Embassy at Tokyo.
From there, on 28 November 1917 (three weeks after
the start of the Russian Revolution), she wrote the
following letter to Lady Fane, in England.

Darling Mother,

... This is the true story of the killing of Rasputin as told
by Yousoupoff himself. It is particularly horrid and
medieval but interesting. I remember first seeing Rasputin
at the tourney when Lady Curzon was Queen of Beauty.
He was so beautiful that I asked who he was.

Rasputin, besides being vicious, was given to drink and
was quite illiterate. He had a fine presence, great physical
strength and a highly-developed magnetic power which
enabled him to cure by the laying on of hands. Though he
had relations with most of the ladies of the court and
society, he was never really more to the Empress and young
Archduchesses than arch-prophet and *hypnotiser*....

Yousoupoff, who is young and handsome and of the
intensely 'Russian' Party, got news at the beginning of
November last year that a separate peace was to be declared
by the Court Party. He could think of no way to prevent
this but by the removal of Rasputin, and set to work to
devise means to remove him. This was extremely difficult
as Rasputin was always shadowed around Saint Petersburg
by his secret police and, suspecting Yousoupoff's clique,
always refused to meet the young man. Finally Yousoupoff
went to one of the court ladies, who had had an affair with
Rasputin, and told her that he, Yousoupoff, was
tuberculous – which he looks – and that having heard of
Rasputin's strange powers, he prayed her to implore
Rasputin's assistance. Finally Rasputin consented, stipulat-
ing that the interview must be at Rasputin's house.

Yousoupoff went on the day appointed, and was told to
undress and lie on a sofa while Rasputin proceeded to make
passes over him. Yousoupoff said that he felt as though

streams of fire were running through him, and he melted like wax except for one square patch of resistance in the middle of his chest. These visits and treatments continued daily for some time, the square of resistance each time increasing till finally Yousoupoff said he felt himself entirely proof against Rasputin's power. During these weeks he laid himself out in every way to fascinate Rasputin, who ended by becoming quite infatuated with him and, being very musical, used to spend hours listening to Yousoupoff's singing and playing — but never forgot himself sufficiently to visit Yousoupoff at his own house or even to accept invitations to Yousoupoff's friends. By this time they were on Christian-name terms and extremely intimate.

The days were passing and Yousoupoff was in despair as he knew Rasputin was leaving for the Crimea in December and he wouldn't get another chance in time to avert the disaster of a separate peace. He made a last appeal to Rasputin, saying he would take offence if he didn't pay him one visit to see his curios, etc., before his departure. To his amazement and joy, Rasputin consented — but only on condition that Yousoupoff's servants were sent away for the night — that no one knew of the visit — that they were entirely alone. . . . Overjoyed, Yousoupoff agreed to everything and dashed off to the Grand Duke Dimitri, who was his great friend and fellow-conspirator. They finally added two more members to the plot — a doctor to prepare the poison (as they had settled that as the easiest way to do the deed) and a member of the Duma — of the right — as a witness.

The evening [of Friday, 16 December] arrived — the servants were dismissed. Yousoupoff went off in his little two-seater car to collect Rasputin. He found him gorgeously dressed in a silk soutane, with a jewelled cross on his chest. He helped him into a big fur-coat and motored him to his house, where he ushered him into the luxurious sitting-room. This room was on the ground floor, filled with objects of art, and had six doors to it. In the middle stood a table with poisoned fruit, cakes and wine at one end, while opposite were corresponding refreshments *not* poisoned. This poison, prepared by the doctor, was supposed to work instantaneously.

They sat down and, pouring out some of the poisoned wine, Yousoupoff handed it to his guest, saying, 'Drink, Gregory, to our next happy meeting.' To his horror, Rasputin refused. He also refused to eat. This was the first time Yousoupoff had known him to refuse a drink, and naturally concluded that the plot was discovered. It wasn't till ages afterwards that he found out that Rasputin belonged to a strange sect which would not eat or drink the first time they crossed the threshold of a house.

Rasputin said, 'Fetch your guitar and play and sing to me, as I cannot remain long.' Yousoupoff played and sang, and Rasputin got more and more fascinated – till suddenly he held out his glass to be filled. Still singing, Yousoupoff filled it and watched him gulp it down. Again and again Rasputin tossed down glassfuls of the poisoned wine and then began eating the poisoned cakes and fruit. Yousoupoff watched anxiously for the expected result and – nothing happened! The hours passed; Rasputin drank and Yousoupoff sang, thinking desperately what could be done, knowing that this night was his last chance. The poison had no effect beyond making Rasputin rather drunk.

Suddenly Yousoupoff thought of a plan. Leaning forward, he said, 'You remember, Gregory, I told you of the fine crucifix I picked up last week and which you haven't seen yet. I simply must show it to you before you leave – just wait a minute while I get it.' He ran upstairs to his bedroom, where the three other conspirators were anxiously waiting and wondering why things took so long. He hurriedly told them what had happened, seized the crucifix and his revolver, and rushed back to find Rasputin leaning in an armchair, half asleep.

Handing Rasputin the crucifix, he said, 'Take it to the light, Gregory, it is a very fine one.' Rasputin rose and, holding the crucifix in both hands up to the lamp, was just saying 'Yes, the expression is . . .' when Yousoupoff shot him through the shoulders from behind. Rasputin fell with a crash. Hearing the shot, the three other men came down, and the doctor said that Rasputin was in his death-agony and could only last a few minutes. Thereupon they left him lying on the floor and all four went up to the bedroom, shutting the door.

All at once they heard a noise, and there was Rasputin covered in blood and foam – on all fours – having crawled up the stairs. He seemed to have superhuman strength. He wrenched the handle of the door and, seeing Yousoupoff, he gathered himself together for a spring – but the Deputy drew his revolver and shot him twice. Yousoupoff then seems to have broken down completely and, throwing himself on the corpse, tore it and mauled it like a dog.

By this time, the secret police were hammering on the door. Yousoupoff and the Deputy sent the Grand Duke down to parley with them. The police asked what the shots were and Dimitri carelessly answered, 'Absolutely nothing – Yousoupoff's dog turned savage and flew at me, so I shot him.' Seeing who it was, the police made no more inquiries and departed. The conspirators then dressed Rasputin in his fur-coat, put the body on a sledge, drove it to the River Neva, broke a hole in the ice and bundled him in – but, in so doing, one of Rasputin's fur boots fell off. This the police found next day, and so recovered the body.

The Empress, on hearing of her favourite's murder, went nearly mad and swore that, when caught, the murderers should be hanged without trial. But Yousoupoff and Dimitri went to the Czar and confessed, and he, worried that he might be implicated, didn't dare to touch them beyond banishing them. The Empress and her Lady-in-Waiting visited the hut on the Neva where Rasputin's body lay and wrapped it in rich silk. The Lady-in-Waiting's name was something like Vourouba.

This account of the macabre incident is from Lady

Muriel Paget, who had it direct from Yousoupoff himself. She arrived here in Tokyo on her way from Russia via Siberia with a troop of nurses and governesses....

Love,
LUCY

EDITOR'S NOTE. None of the murderers was tried for the crime; but, as has been said, the Tsar ordered the banishment of two of them — Yousoupoff to his estates in the province of Kursk, north of the Ukraine (where he remained but a short while before becoming an émigré).

The Gutteridge Murder

W. TEIGNMOUTH SHORE

EARLY ON THE MORNING of Tuesday, 27 September 1927, William Ward, the driver of a van carrying mail, set out from Romford to Abridge, both in the county of Essex, north-east of London. About six o'clock, near Howe Green on the Romford Ongar Road, he came to a bend, and on turning the corner saw on his right hand a huddled form lying against the hedge. It was the body of Police Constable George Gutteridge. Quoting Mr Ward:

> I then got out. He was lying in a sort of semi-sitting position, resting against the bank. His left hand was closed. I took hold of his hand and it was cold. In his right hand there was a pencil. I also noted a pocket-book on the ground, and his helmet. I immediately went to a cottage nearby and fetched the occupier....
> Later on, I telephoned to Romford Police Station.

On receipt of this message, Detective Inspector John Crockford of the Essex Constabulary drove to the spot. This is what he observed:

> I noticed a pocket-book lying close to the body. A little farther on, his helmet was lying in the road. I noticed blood on the road. The blood started six feet from the rear side of the road as you go up-hill [that is, towards Ongar] till you came to the deceased's head. It was a continuous trail of blood. At the place where the head itself lay, there was a pool of blood. There was no entry in the pocket-book relating to what had occurred. The constable was wearing his cape ....

The two buttons of his tunic were undone, and his
whistle was hanging from his pocket on its chain . . . .
His pencil was in his right hand between his thumb
and finger . . . . His truncheon was in his truncheon-
pocket on his right-hand side. His torch was also in his
pocket . . . .

Dr Robert Woodhouse was summoned from Romford,
arriving at about nine o'clock.

Police Constable Gutteridge, a member of the Essex
Constabulary, was stationed at Stapleford Abbotts, living
there with his wife Rose. On the foggy night of Monday,
26 September, he was on duty, and went out again early the
following morning, to meet Constable Sydney Taylor,
who was stationed at Lambourne End, at a 'conference
point' outside Grove House, close by Howe Green. They
met at three o'clock, parting about half an hour later, each
going in the direction of his home. Howe Green is in a
quiet country neighbourhood, with few houses; the road is
unlit and little frequented at night by passenger or
vehicular traffic.

It was decided by the Chief Constable of Essex to ask the
assistance of New Scotland Yard, particularly as the crime
had been committed close on the boundary of the
Metropolitan Police district, and as there was therefore a
considerable probability that the murderer or murderers
would have come from and returned to London. The
Commissioner of the Police of the Metropolis immediately
dispatched Chief Inspector James Berrett and Detective
Sergeant John Harris of the CID, who arrived on the scene
early in the afternoon.

Medical Evidence

The testimony of Doctor Woodhouse was as follows:

I was called to the spot where PC Gutteridge's body
was lying at about nine o'clock in the morning. . . .
Life was extinct when I arrived. As far as I can judge,
he had been dead between four and five hours.

The next day I made a post-mortem examination. There were altogether seven wounds in the head. As far as I could see, there were four entrance wounds and three exit wounds. The four entrance wounds have been divided into two groups, those in the cheek and those through the eyes, two of each.

With regard to the wounds through the cheek, it was the left cheek, and they were on a line with the lobe of the ear, one an inch and a quarter from the lobe of the ear, and the other three-quarters of an inch from the lobe of the ear. As regards the one which was farthest from the lobe of the ear, I was able to trace the exit; I was able to pass a probe through it out at the other side. The exit was at the level of the ear, about an inch in front of it, the track of that wound having risen one inch. It had gone through the palate and out through the jaw-bone at the side, fracturing it as it came out. The wound taken by itself would not necessarily have been fatal. As regards the second wound, the wound nearer the ear, I also tried that wound with a probe and found that it came out on the right side of the neck two inches below the mastoid process[1] on the right side.... This second wound in its passage cut through the right internal carotid artery, and death from that wound would have taken place, very probably in the space of a minute or a minute and a half, from haemorrhage. It is the sort of wound from which the blood would be spurting.... The skin round the wounds showed a large number of small black specks.

There was a wound in each eye, through each eyelid, the one on the right being a trifle higher than the one on the left. The actual skin of the eyelids was broken as if something had been driven through it, and there was what I should call 'peppering' round the wounds. It was the same on both sides of the face, only it was more marked in the case of the right eye than the left. They were bullet-wounds, somewhat oval in shape and scorched round the edges. That was

---

1. The portion of bone projecting behind the ear.

in addition to the black marks I have referred to. I was only able to trace the exit wound of the wound in the right eye, and it came out through a large wound in the back of the head. In the case of the left eye, the probe would not go through it; it came to a dead stop. Later I examined the brain, and found a distorted bullet. It was on the left side of the brain. That is consistent with its being the bullet which went through the eye....

In my opinion, death was due to haemorrhage and lacerations of the brain caused by bullets.

The doctor added that the bullets which made the cheek-wounds had been fired at a distance of about ten inches.

We are now at this: we know the cause of death and have certain clues which indicate what probably took place. Gutteridge seemingly had blown his whistle, possibly hoping that Constable Taylor was still within hearing of it. He had been about to make some notes in his book. There were no signs of a struggle, but on the bank opposite to where the body lay were marks of the tyres of a motor-car that had partly left the roadway.

Bearing all these points in mind, it appeared probable that the constable had been shot by the occupant or occupants of a car which he had stopped, desiring to make some inquiry. As he lay dying, the shots had been fired into his eyes, an act of brutality and ruthlessness which suggested the work of a hardened criminal.

Theft of the Car

That same night – or rather, morning – a Morris-Cowley car had been stolen at Billericay, about twelve miles from the scene of the murder. Was that the car which Gutteridge had challenged? If so, what was it that had made the people in it so vindictive and desperate? About half-past two, this car had been taken from the garage of Doctor Lovell at Billericay. Five hours later, it was discovered, abandoned, at Brixton, South London. A resident there, in Foxley

Road, was in the habit of leaving home at about 7.30am, going out by the back door through a little passage-way shut off from the road by iron gates. This morning he was surprised to find a Morris-Cowley car drawn up close to the house-wall. As he went round the front of the car, he put his hand on the radiator and found it quite warm. Returning in the evening about six and finding the car still there, he communicated with the police. The number on the car proved it to be that which had been stolen from Billericay.

The doctor's two cases of instruments and a small case containing a few drugs were gone. A further and most important point was this : the doctor estimated that when the car left his garage, the mileometer's terminal figures must have been 40.9. The terminal figures at Brixton read 84.3; therefore the car must have been driven some 42 miles. Was there any route from Billericay that would fit these figures?

The distance the car had travelled showed that the direct route from Billericay to London had not been followed, presumably because the thief or thieves desired to avoid Brentwood High Street, where a police officer, on duty all night, might stop them and ask awkward questions. Stage by stage, the route was traced: on past Gutteridge's house; again it was heard close to the scene of the murder; after that, stage by stage, to London. The circuitous ways taken on this foggy night proved that the driver must have intimate knowledge of the countryside. So to Brixton. It is worth quoting here the evidence by Detective Sergeant Harris at the trial:

> On 9 February I went from the address in Brixton, 21 Foxley Road, to Billericay, to Doctor Lovell's house. It was a test-drive with regard to the mileage from this place to the doctor's house. On the first journey we went by the main road, passing through Romford and Brentford, turning off at Shenfield. That is the most direct route we could discover, going by main roads. The mileage was exactly 27 miles. Before we made the

return journey, we set the mileometer at zero, and returned to the place we had started from by quite another route. On that occasion we went down the Mountnessing Road past the spot where Gutteridge's body was found, and thence, via Abridge, Chigwell, Buckhurst Hill and Woodford, to Stratford, and we there rejoined the main road and travelled the same route as before, continuing to Aldgate and the Elephant and Castle to Foxley Road. When we stopped at Foxley Road, the mileage was 42.1 miles.

On the offside running board of the stolen car, adjacent to the driver's seat, were a number of small red stains, which on analysis proved to be human blood. Under the front seats, an empty cartridge case was found. It was stamped 'Mark IV' and was of a kind that had been withdrawn from the army towards the end of 1914. Examination of the dead man had shown that one of the bullets causing the eye-wounds had been propelled by black powder, an explosive that had not been used for many years for army ammunition. Would the owner of the pistol from which that cartridge had been fired be found in possession of similar ammunition?

Collecting Evidence

Until the end of a case such as this, it cannot be known what facts will prove to be specially significant. Therefore, every one must be observed, noted, and considered. Information must be patiently collected, studied, recorded. There must be untiring patience in the pursuit.

It need scarcely be said that much time and energy were spent and wasted by the police in examining every particle of information volunteered, only too often by well-meaning people. Several hundred persons were interviewed; their statements were recorded and checked. Every circumstance that might have a bearing on the case was carefully looked into, including recent purchases of arms and the comings and goings of suspicious persons. Of course, there were bogus confessions. Criminals whose records suggested that they could be guilty of such a crime were looked up, and inquiries made as to what they had been doing on the night of the murder. A house-to-house search in Brixton produced no result. Fingerprints on the steering-wheel of the stolen car were of no assistance; nor were those on the door of the garage at Billericay. But there were suspicions, which centred on a man who knew the highways and byways through which the car had been driven and whose reputation as a desperado was notorious.

Towards the end of December, valuable information did come to hand, from Sheffield. A letter was received at Scotland Yard from an ex-convict who had known a man named Browne at Dartmoor, and who stated that Browne was the driver of a car which had been the cause of a serious accident in Sheffield on 14 November. Browne was wanted by the police there on a summons for reckless driving. The driver's licence ran thus: 'Sidney Rhodes, 27 York Terrace, Clapham Road, Stockwell, S.W.', which proved to be false. Inquiries showed that the driver was Frederick Guy Browne, who had sold in Sheffield a car that he had stolen in Tooting and who was conducting an apparently legitimate business in a garage at Battersea. The informant described Browne as a most dangerous man – which was not news to Scotland Yard. He also said that, when visiting Browne in his garage in October, he had seen a big Webley revolver hanging in the office there and that he had jestingly said to Browne and his assistant, one Pat Kennedy: 'I hope you didn't shoot Gutteridge' – to which Browne had airily replied: 'We have been expecting them coming for us every day. But if they do come, we can prove we were letting cars out of the garage at 6am. We did go down there for a car the day before this chap was murdered, and it is a good job we were not there the same day.' Later, in November, at the informant's home in Sheffield, Browne 'stood in the corner of my kitchen with a large Webley in each hand, which were loaded, and he held them up and said: "If they come to my garage I shall let them in even if there is half a dozen or a dozen, but there is not one that goes out alive. I shall get the first car afterwards, and clear".' During this visit he was alleged to have said: 'The police are not so fond of pulling a car up at night after what we did to Gutteridge.'

Benjamin Stow, a butcher at Sheffield, was acquainted with Browne and had bought a car from him in November, paying for it partly in cash and partly by exchanging an Angus-Sanderson car. The purchased car was the one that had been stolen from a garage at Tooting.

On Wednesday morning, 18 January, Browne set out in the Angus-Sanderson to meet a friend who was being released from Dartmoor and to whom he intended to offer a job in his garage. That Browne was absent was discovered by the police, who lay in wait for his return in considerable numbers, expecting a desperate resistance unless they could catch the man unawares.

It will be well now to explore the careers of these two men, Browne and Kennedy.

Frederick Guy Browne, or Leo Browne, was born in 1881 of working-class parents. Nothing significant is known of his boyhood. In 1909 he was at Eynsham, in Oxfordshire, conducting a bicycle-repairing business and practising bicycle-stealing. During 1910–1913, he was convicted for carrying firearms, for larceny, and for burglary. Toward the close of 1916 he joined the army and was stationed with the Royal Engineers at Longmoor Camp, Hampshire, working in the railway-operating department. Early in 1918 he was sentenced at Petersfield to ten months' imprisonment, and was discharged from the army in November with an 'indifferent' character. Late in 1921, he was living at Eastwood, near Southend, and during his residence there he became familiar with the countryside between Billericay and London. On Christmas Eve, 1923, he was arrested, charged with making fraudulent claims upon insurance companies, and in the following February was sentenced to four years' penal servitude. At Parkhurst

Prison his behaviour was so disorderly and violent that he was transferred to Dartmoor, where it is said that he first met Kennedy. He came out on 30 March 1927, having served the whole of his term, as he did not wish to have to report to the police after his release.

He set up business in a garage in Battersea, doing lawful work in the letting of lock-up garages, car-repairing, and so forth. He was an excellent mechanic. He also did unlawful work. In 1927 he participated in a profitable burglary, the looting of the railway station, Tooting Junction; as we already know, he stole the car that he sold at Sheffield; also, he stole a Singer car at Tooting, and in December he and another broke into the railway station at Eynsham, coming away with considerable booty; he subsequently stole a Buick at Harringay and raided the railway station at Borden in Hampshire. He was a man of marked muscular power, which he sometimes boastingly displayed by raising a car without the aid of a jack. He was a teetotaller and a non-smoker.

Patrick Michael William, or William Henry, Kennedy was born in 1891 or 1892 in Ayrshire, his parents being Irish. All his life he spoke with an Irish brogue. When a lad, he was taken to Liverpool, where he was apprenticed to a compositor. From 1903 to 1911 he served in the army with discredit, and in 1913 returned to Liverpool. His criminal career was not romantic; indecent exposure, petty thefts, 'drunk and disorderly', housebreaking, and larceny exhausted his abilities. Yet again he entered the army, from which he was eventually discharged with ignominy; he then returned to Liverpool and resumed his career of crimes. According to his own account, it was in June or July 1927 that he joined Browne, leaving him in December.

Arrest of Browne

Returning to town on 20 January, and after dropping his friend not far from Scotland Yard, where he had to report, Browne drove to his garage, which he reached at about

7.30pm. He was promptly arrested, no chance being given him for resistance. He was held on the charge of stealing a car; but it quickly became apparent that there was more than sufficient evidence to justify his being charged with the murder of Constable Gutteridge.

It is not necessary to do more than indicate the general nature of the evidence which Browne had stored up. When searched, in his pocket was found a Spencer-Wells forceps, which he said he had possessed for a long time. In the office were more instruments, bandages, and so forth, exactly such things as had been in the two small attaché cases which Doctor Lovell had left in his car. The doctor had no doubt that they, and other things found at Browne's lodgings, were his property. In Browne's hip-pocket were found cartridges, of which one was a Mark IV. In a compartment beside the driver's seat in the car was a Webley service revolver, fully loaded with six Mark IV cartridges. In the garage office were more of them, and still more were found at Browne's home. Later, another Webley was discovered in the car.

Kennedy and his Statement

Hearing of Browne's arrest, Kennedy thought it would be wise to retire to Liverpool, where on 25 January he was arrested. He was brought to London, to Scotland Yard, where he was seen by Chief Inspector Berrett, who said to him: 'You are detained on a charge of being concerned with stealing a Vauxhall car. And I have been making inquiries for some time past respecting the murder of PC Gutteridge. Can you give me any information about that occurrence?' To which Kennedy replied: 'I may be able to tell you something, but let me consider,' adding after a little while: 'Can I see my wife?' She came to him, and he said to her: 'When I was arrested in Liverpool yesterday, I told you there was something more serious at the back of it. Well, there is. These officers are making inquiries about that policeman who was murdered in Essex.'

179

'You didn't murder him, did you?' she asked him.

'No, I didn't; but I was there and know who did. If I'm charged with the murder and found guilty, I shall be hanged, and you will be a widow. On the other hand, if I'm charged and found guilty of being an accessory after the fact, I shall receive a severe sentence of penal servitude and be a long time from you. Will you wait for me?'

'Yes, love, I'll wait for you any time. . . . Tell these gentlemen the truth of what took place.'

'All right, I will.' Then to Inspector Berrett: 'You can take down what I want to say and I'll sign it.'

He proceeded to make a statement which, though lengthy, must be quoted nearly in full:

New Scotland Yard
26 January 1928

WILLIAM HENRY KENNEDY, no fixed abode, Compositor, age 37,
WHO SAITH:
. . . I have tonight, 26 January 1928, at 8pm, been interviewed by Chief Inspector Berrett, and told he is making inquiries respecting the murder of PC Gutteridge at Stapleford Abbotts, Essex, on the morning of 27 September 1927, and asked if I can give any information respecting it. I wish voluntarily to tell you what I know about the matter, having been cautioned that what I do say will be taken down in writing and may be given in evidence.

Signed W. KENNEDY

At the end of either June or July, whilst I was at work on a farm at Cheshire, after my release from prison in November 1926, I received a letter from a man known as Fred Browne, which letter I have destroyed or handed to the representative of the Central Association[1] in Liverpool.

In the letter he told me he was just starting a garage in

1. The Discharged Prisoners' Association.

Battersea — 7a Northcote Road — and invited me to come down and act as manager. . . . He said he could not offer me much money at first, but it would cost me nothing for board and lodgings, as I could live at the garage. . . . I came to London and slept on the premises at 7a Northcote Road, at the back of the place used as an office. My duties consisted of attending to correspondence, keeping the books, making and dealing with accounts. The man Fred Browne was also sleeping on the premises at the time. After this had been going on, I think, till about the end of August, Browne went to live with his wife at 2 Huguenot Place.

I remained sleeping at the garage till December, and used to go out on occasions on motor-rides with Browne, on ordinary and various business journeys, and once or twice we called at his sister's place at Buckhurst Hill.

I well remember the day of 26 September. He suggested that I should accompany him to Billericay, to assist him in stealing a 'Raleigh' car at the end of the High Street, away from the station. We went to a place which faces a large, empty house standing in its own grounds. Browne entered the grounds of the house where the Raleigh car was supposed to be. We went to Billericay by rail from Liverpool Street, which I think was shortly after 7pm, because we left the garage [Browne's] at 6.30pm.

I accompanied Browne into the grounds. Browne opened the door of the garage, I think with a key, and examined the Raleigh car, and we then left the garage and grounds and hid in the grounds of the empty house and waited until the people owning the Raleigh car went to bed.

Browne told me to wait in the grounds of the empty house, and Browne went to the garage where the car was stored. A dog came out and, starting to bark, it made Browne leave and join me, and he said: 'It's no good here. We can't get back by train, so we'll try somewhere else.' The time was then, I should think, about 11pm. We walked through the village again and came to a spot, which I now know is the doctor's house, on a sharp bend — at the opposite end to where the Raleigh car was, and on the main London Road.

We saw the garage at the end of the doctor's house, and we went into the field opposite, and sat on some old palings or gates, and waited till the lights went out in the doctor's house. It was getting late, and must have been after midnight.

After the lights went out, Browne and I went to the garage, which is a wood structure, and he forced the doors with, I think, a small tyre lever or tool of some kind, which he took with him. The door was opened easily. He first examined the petrol tank and make of car, and told me there was plenty of petrol in the tank. He told me it was a Morris-Cowley. It ran down on its own weight to the road, and we pushed it along about a hundred yards in the opposite direction, or at right angles to the main road. Browne said: 'We will go by the byways and escape the main road.' We then went for a long run round country lanes at great pace at different times. We got to several crossroads and corners, where it was necessary for us to examine the sign-posts, but eventually we got on to a kind of main road on the way to Ongar. When we got some distance up on this road we saw someone who stood on the bank and flashed his lamp as a signal to stop. We drove on, and I then heard a police-whistle, and told Browne to stop. He did so quite willingly, and when the person came up we saw it was a policeman. Browne was driving, and I was sitting on his left in the front. The policeman came up close to the car and stood near Browne and asked him where he was going and where he came from. Browne told him we came from Lea Bridge Road Garage, and had been out to do some repairs. The policeman then asked him if he had a card. Browne said, 'No.' He then asked Browne, 'Have you a driver's licence?' Browne again said, 'No.' The policeman then again asked him where he came from, and Browne stammered in his answer, and the policeman then said, 'Is the car yours?' I then said, 'No; the car is mine.' The policeman flashed his light in both our faces, and was at this time standing close to the running board on the offside, and then asked me if I knew the number of the car, and Browne said, 'You'll see it on the front of the car.' The policeman said, 'I know the number, but do you?' I said, 'Yes, I can give you the number,' and said 'TW 6120.' He said, 'Very well, I'll take particulars,' put his torch back in his pocket, and pulled out his notebook, and was in the act of writing when I heard a report, quickly followed by another one. I saw the policeman stagger back and fall over by the bank at the hedge. I said to Browne, 'What have you done?' and then saw he had a large Webley revolver in his hand. He said, 'Get out quick.' I immediately got out and went round to the policeman, who was lying on his back, and Browne came over and said, 'I'll finish the – ,' and I said, 'For God's sake don't shoot any more, the man's dying,' as he was groaning.

The policeman's eyes were open, and Browne, addressing him, said, 'What are you looking at me like that for?' and, stooping down, shot him at close range through both eyes. There were only four shots fired. Browne then said, 'Let's get back into the car.' We had driven close into the bank, and backed out a little, and drove on in the direction of Ongar. He gave me the revolver and told me to load it while he drove on. I loaded it, and in my excitement I dropped an empty shell in the car. The other three I threw away into the roads. We drove at great pace through many villages, the names of which I do not know, but I know we went through Buckhurst Hill, and then Bow and the Elephant and Castle, and while on this journey Browne said, 'Have you loaded that gun again? If you have, give it me back.'

I gave it to him, and he kept it on the seat by his right-hand side. He wanted to take the car to the garage, but I persuaded him to have nothing to do with the garage. We drove to Brixton, and went up a road I don't know the name of, and drove into a *cul-de-sac* at about 5.30am. We left the car and came out into the main road, and came by tramcar back to the garage, bringing with us two cases out of the car containing doctor's instruments. These, or the majority of them, were smashed up, and the cases were cut up into small pieces, which Browne later took out in his car and distributed about various roads in the country, so as to destroy all evidence, and I did not know that he retained any of the doctor's property. I forgot to mention that on our journey, after shooting the policeman, Browne turned into a tree owing to fog at a gate. The fog was very dense at that time. I think he damaged the near-side front wing. I was very excited at the time. We returned to the garage about 6am, and commenced our work.

Dyson[1] arrived at his usual time, about 8am, and business carried on as usual. I suggested to Browne that we should go right away from London, as I knew inquiries were sure to be made. Browne said there was no danger, and induced me to stop, and said if I made up my mind to leave him he would blow my brains out. He had the Webley revolver in his hand when he said this, and, as I knew it was loaded, I thought he would. I then later went to a newspaper shop and purchased the various editions of the papers, and in one I found that Scotland Yard was supposed to have found fingerprints, and again wanted to leave, and he said, 'No, you don't; you'll stop here and face it out with me. If anyone comes up here, there will be a shooting match.' . . .

In December I told Browne I was going away, and he made no objection then, and drove me to Euston in the car about, I think, 17 December 1927.

I then went to West Kirby to an address I don't want to mention, and remained until 13 January last, when I returned to London with a woman whom I have married, and I have lived at 2 Huguenot Place till last Saturday, 21 January 1928, when I left and went again back to Liverpool, where I was arrested. Since I came to London on 13 January I have called at the garage on two occasions, and he said, 'Hullo, you've come back.' On the first occasion no mention was made of the crime.

On 17 January 1928 – a Tuesday – he wanted me to go to Devonshire with him in a car, but my wife persuaded me not to, and told me that, whatever he was going for, I was better out of it. I think Browne went, and I left.

I went to the garage again at 2pm, Saturday, 21 January 1928, and when I got to the entrance I found the gate locked, and saw two men who I took to be detectives, and suspected something was wrong. I went to my wife and told her to pack, as we were going away, giving her no reason. I went to Clapham Common and sent a bogus telegram to myself saying someone was ill. This was an excuse I made to explain our leaving.

1. Employed by Browne as a general handyman.

The Hand of God or Somebody

James Berry PUBLIC EXECUTIONER FROM 1884 TO 1892

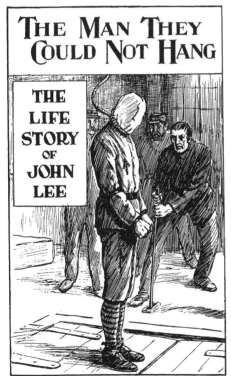

THE MAN THEY COULD NOT HANG

THE LIFE STORY OF JOHN LEE

PUBLISHED AT 17 AND 18, HENRIETTA STREET, LONDON, W.C.

The Protracted Murder
of Gregory Rasputin

Rasputin

Prince Yousoupoff and his wife, Princess Irina

The Gutteridge Murder

Browne's 'living-room', where he was arrested

Daily Mirror

THE DAILY PICTURE — NEWSPAPER WITH THE LARGEST NET SALE

No. 7,639 — Registered at the G.P.O. as a Newspaper — SATURDAY, APRIL 28, 1928 — One Penny

BROWNE AND KENNEDY SENTENCED TO DEATH

Mr. Justice Avory, who sentenced Browne and Kennedy to death. The trial lasted five days.

William Henry Kennedy.

Frederick Guy Browne.

Dr. Woolhouse, a witness.

Mrs. Gutteridge wept bitterly in the box.

The children of the murdered constable—William, aged four, and Muriel, aged twelve.

The spot on a lonely country road near Stapleford Abbots, Essex, where Police Constable Gutteridge was found shot dead on September 27 last. Inset, the murdered policeman,— and another photograph of Browne.

I have seen Browne in possession of two Webley revolvers, which were always kept loaded, and he had plenty of ammunition. He also told me he had a Smith & Wesson, but I never saw it. I believe he kept it at home. He also had a small nickel .22 revolver, which was also kept at home.

I have been worried ever since the murder of the constable, and at times I became desperate, expecting I should be arrested, and not knowing what to do.

I have made this statement quite voluntarily, after being cautioned, and am prepared to give it in a court of law if necessary.

It has been read over to me, and all I have stated is the whole truth of what took place on the night of 26–27 September 1927.

Signed W. KENNEDY

Though a statement made to the police is worth little or nothing until much or all of it has been checked and corroborated, it is easy to imagine with what eagerness and keen attention this one was heard – then considered almost word by word. How much or how little of it was true? From information already in hand, it seemed likely that most of it was fact.

Obviously Kennedy felt that the net was closing tightly round him and believed that the only way for him to escape the gallows was to incriminate himself up to a point, while endeavouring to lay the heavier burden of guilt upon Browne. But he overlooked the fact, of which he afterwards felt the full force, that he was not the less a murderer even if he had not fired a shot.

Some of his statement could not be checked; much was closely followed up. Whether the two did or did not travel to Billericay from Liverpool Street at or about 7pm did not much matter. As regards the attempt to steal the Raleigh car, which was interrupted by the barking of a dog, that assertion was substantiated in a somewhat curious way. At the trial, one of the witnesses, a domestic servant employed by a resident in Southend Road, Billericay, said: 'Mr Pitcher has a Raleigh motor-car, which he keeps in his garage near his house. I remember the night Police Constable Gutteridge was shot. The car was in the garage that night. The door was not locked with a key, just shut. We do not have a dog in the house, but a dog comes every night round to the dustbin in the garden.'

It was known that Browne's advice: 'We will go by the byways and escape the main road' was acted on and that they did get on to the Romford Ongar Road. As to the exact incidents of the murdering, no one will ever learn the full truth. It does not matter who fired the shots. The original of the bogus telegram was produced and proved to be in Kennedy's handwriting.

His statement, or confession as it may well be called, could not be used as evidence against Browne; only against himself if proved to be true. All that was needed to hang him was to prove that he had been Browne's companion and accomplice; his statement provided almost all the necessary evidence.

Evidence against Browne

It had to be proved that Browne also was in that car, and Browne had provided the necessary evidence. The doctor's stolen instruments were found in Browne's possession. Browne had used words, when arrested, which, if not conclusively incriminating, were at least highly suspicious. When charging the jury at the trial, Mr Justice Avory said:

> The inspector who had Browne in charge on that evening, and who, as you know, had charged him only with stealing a Vauxhall car, found in Browne's pocket a driver's licence in the name of Frederick Harris, and Browne said, 'That is a dud in case I am stopped.' The inspector adds that when they found in Browne's trousers pocket twelve cartridges, service cartridges, which can be fired from a Webley revolver, Browne said, 'That's done it; now you have found them, it's all up with me,' nothing at that time having been said about any crime of violence. And they

found in his pocket a mask, which was produced, and Browne said, 'There you are, you have got it now; that's the lot, you won't find anything else.' It was then that Detective Bevis came in with the 'new' Webley revolver in his hand and the six cartridges which he had taken out of it, and Detective Bevis said, 'I have just found this fully loaded in the off-side pocket by the driver's seat of the Angus car outside,' and Browne said, 'You have found that, have you? I am done for now.' Hawkyard, another detective, has sworn he heard Browne say, 'That's done it; now you have found them, it's all up with me.' And when the mask was found, he said, 'There you are, you have got the lot now.' And when Bevis brought in the revolver, Browne said, 'Now you have found that, I am done for.' And, at nine o'clock that evening, Browne said, 'How many of you were there? All you lot to pinch me? It's a good job you didn't collar me when I was in the car or some of you would have gone west, and me after you. I have seen a man shoot six down with a gun like that, and you can take it from me that they didn't get up.' Bevis also heard Browne say, when the nickel-plated revolver was produced, 'That's no good, it would only tickle unless it hit you in a vital part. If you had stopped me in the car, I would have shot five of you and saved one for myself.' And later on he heard him say, 'From what I can see of it, I shall have to get a machine-gun for you bastards next time.' Now, those things are the things alleged to have been said by Browne at the time when he was found in possession of at least four revolvers, all fully loaded, and, in view of those statements – in view of the statements that he is prepared to shoot down anybody who attempts to stop him when he is in the car – you must judge whether you believe him when he says in that witness-box that he has never fired a revolver in his life, and that he only keeps them loaded in order to prevent them going rusty. Browne has disputed that he said some of these things; he has admitted that he said others of them; and the explanation which is offered to you of his saying the others is that he thought at the time that he might be charged with being unlawfully in possession of firearms without a licence. It is for you to judge whether you think that affords a reasonable explanation of the statements that he made − 'It is all up with me', 'I am done for now' − fearing he is simply going to be charged with an offence for which he is liable to a fine.

The use of those questionable words and the possession of the doctor's property, severally or taken together, would not have justified a verdict of guilty against Browne. But, in conjunction with his being in possession of the revolver from which was fired the cartridge-case found in the car and of unusual ammunition of the same kind as that with which Constable Gutteridge was slain, the possibility of mere coincidence was wiped out. The innocent accumulation of coincidence upon coincidence does not happen outside fiction.

When asked to account for the Webley revolver, Browne declared that he had never fired it and that he had bought it in April 1927 at Tilbury Docks from a sailor whose name he did not know and whom he could not describe; he had obtained the ammunition from a man he knew in the army whom he did not wish to name. In his statement, from which the above assertions are taken, he went on to say:

Shortly after I got the revolver it began to go rusty, but I kept it well oiled. I have never used it. I loaded it so that it would frighten anyone in case they interfered with me, and the reason I carried the weapon was because at the beginning of the War, when I was working for Pytchley Auto Car Co, Great Portland Street, W., delivering cars by road in different parts of the country, on two occasions − once when I was going through Gloucester to South Wales − a man at dusk signalled to me when I was driving the car to stop. As I slowed down in accordance with his signal, and I was engaged on the near-side speaking to him, two other men jumped on the off-side running board and demanded money. I was unprepared, and gave them what little money I had. Some six weeks after that occasion, when going to Bournemouth with another car, the same kind of thing happened to me, with a man calling on me to stop, but I declined on this occasion to stop. After this second occasion I made up my mind to be armed when taking cars to the country, and I purchased a revolver with a long barrel, but I had no ammunition.

I later joined the army, but have never been threatened since. I remarked on the revolver to my firm when I got back, but not to the police, and the reason I had it on me today was because I had been on a country run to Devon.

As the Solicitor-General put it at the trial: 'Remember that this cartridge was the comparatively rare Mark IV, and ask yourself this question: "How does Browne account for the possession of that weapon, how does he account for the possession of that rare sort of ammunition, some of which was used in the perpetration of the murder, except on the footing of his own complicity in the murder?"'

Bullets of an unusual character had been discovered in and near the body of the murdered man. An empty cartridge-case from which one of those bullets had been fired had been found in the doctor's car. Browne possessed the Webley revolver from which that cartridge had been fired. Robert Churchill, the fire-arms expert, stated at the trial: 'The cap of the cartridge takes the imprint of the breech-shield of the revolver, and under microscopic examination it is possible for me to see that this particular cartridge was fired from this Webley revolver, and could not have been fired from any other revolver.' Also, the Chief Examiner at the Royal Small Arms Factory, Enfield Lock, examined the cartridge-case and compared it with the breech-shield of the Webley revolver. When asked, 'Does the examination enable you to express an opinion as to the revolver with which that cartridge was fired?' he replied: 'Not only an opinion – I say that case was fired from that revolver.' And in answer to this question, from the Judge, 'You mean to say that without doubt?' he answered: 'Absolutely.'

We have followed this crime-story from the finding of the body of the murdered constable to the discovery of the damning evidence against Browne and Kennedy, who were tried at the Central Criminal Court on Monday, 23 April 1928, and succeeding days. The jury returned a verdict of Guilty of what was rightly described as 'a most foul and brutal murder'.

Highly-coloured melodrama flooded the press while the murderers were awaiting execution: letters, confessions, poems, memoirs, and much descriptive matter, in which fragments of truth were swamped by masses of fiction. These productions have little historical value, and therefore do not concern us.

On Thursday, 31 May, at 9am, Browne was executed at Pentonville Prison and Kennedy at Wandsworth.

Editor's Explanation

Readers who have read few books of this sort will probably be wondering why an account of the Gutteridge case appears in this one; readers versed in the true-crime genre may be wondering why I chose to use an account that makes no specific reference to a matter that, because it is picturesque, is remembered after the facts of the case are forgotten. I guess that Teignmouth Shore, undoubtedly aware of the matter, lumped it with other 'productions' that, in his penultimate paragraph, he consigned to a trash-can labelled 'Highly-Coloured Melodrama'; − sub-labelled 'Productions [in which] fragments of truth were swamped by masses of fiction'.

I have written elsewhere that 'legend is more pliable, and therefore more durable, than truth' − and that aphorism, needing supportive evidence, receives some in the form of the Gutteridge matter, which is certainly a concoction, and which seems to have been concocted shortly after the trial of Browne and Kennedy by a shameless journalist in the pay of a national paper. I say *seems* because many national-newspaper stories blazoned as being **EXCLUSIVE!** are nothing of the kind: often, main parts of a so-called scoop have been pinched from or inspired by a modest 'filler' in an earlier edition of a rival paper – or, more likely, of a paper so limited in its circulation that it provides no competition at all. Unless a researcher is so stupidly diligent as to scour every apt earlier edition of every paper, not excepting the *South-East Huntingdon Bugle*, it is quite as stupid of him to insist that a story appeared, entirely new, uniquely in a particular paper on a particular day.

By 1969 (actually, long before – but never mind), the Gutteridge *figment* had become An Acknowledged Fact. On 16 July of that year, *The Times* of London, a 'newspaper of record', noted the death of a detective involved in the Gutteridge investigation – and stated that:

> *Brown* [sic] *and Kennedy, fearing that their image would remain 'photographed' on the pupils of the dead policeman, shot out his eyes.*

Whoever invented the superstitious reason for Browne's or Kennedy's post-murder act was not so creative as to have invented the superstition. The retina-retention notion was at least a hundred years old in 1928. At some time during those years, it had been given a pseudo-scientific fillip by a German laboratory-worker who said that he thought he had seen a likeness of the flame of his bunsen-burner on the retina of a frog that he had just killed on behalf of science.

Seven and a bit years before the murder of Constable Gutteridge, the retina-retention notion had been publicised – uncontemptuously – by the *Times* of New York, apropos of the murder of Joseph Bowne Elwell, whose first claim to fame was as the foremost bridge-player of his time, and who had also received notice as a daring gambler on the stock exchange, the owner of a string of race-horses, a developer of real-estate in Florida, an unofficial 'spy-catcher', a dealer in bootleg booze, and, ever since he had separated from his wife, an industrious philanderer – his eligibility as a grass-bachelor enhanced by the loveliness of his hair and the dazzling perfection of his teeth.

191

Early in the morning of Friday, 11 June 1920, Elwell's daily-woman let herself in to his fine house on West Seventieth Street, Manhattan – and found him sitting in a throne-like chair, dying from a gunshot wound through his cranium. She didn't recognise him at first, for he was as bald as a coot, and the gaping of his mouth revealed that he had only three teeth, none contiguous. That slight who-he? mystery was explained before the case became one of murder, Elwell having died without saying a word: an investigator, traipsing around Elwell's bedroom, noticed an expensive bespoke wig on a block and a complicated dentural contraption in a glass of water.

Chiefly because of an excess of investigative groups, each working in rivalry with the others, and each more anxious to prevent any of the rival groups from succeeding than to succeed themselves, nearly all of the other mysteries remained mysterious – among those, the three main ones: what was the motive for the murder?... who had committed it? ... how had that person managed to get undamagingly into the house, the outer doors of which were locked, the downstairs windows of which were covered with grilles, the skylight of which was covered with an iron frame?

What with all the wild surmise about Elwell's 'harem', his discarded (and therefore, of course, revengeful) lady-friends, the devoted husbands he had cuckolded, the business associates and bootleggers and gamblers who had either owed him vast sums or been owed vast sums by him, foreign (and no doubt Bolshevik) agents, *et al*, there was great public interest in the case. On 16 June, a member of the local *Times* Brigade, ordered to gather 'all the [Elwell] news that was fit to print', reported on a claustrophobic time he had had the day before, under the heading **25,000 JAM ELWELL BLOCK**. The number does not seem to have been a misprint, for, as you will see, it also appeared in the report; but one is dubious of the reporter's arithmetic: even if there was an 0 too many, that would still have crammed very large crowds into quite a small area. Here is the report:

About 25,000 persons yesterday visited the block in West Seventieth Street between Broadway and West End Avenue, where the Elwell house is located. Several traffic patrolmen were on duty at both ends of the block to regulate the motor cars attracted to the neighbourhood of the murder.

The detectives have been consistently annoyed with all sorts of cranks going to the house to volunteer their services in solving the mystery.... A woman of sixty, who told the detectives she had come all the way from Chicago because she was interested in the case, advised them to pin their faith in the ouija board and employ it until the mystery was solved....

One man, a doctor, ninety-four years old, who refused to give his name, spends most of each day in front of the house in company with newspapermen.

In my book *The Slaying of Joseph Bowne Elwell*,[1] I reprinted that report, and then commented:

Murder cases have a way of enlisting persons with Bunyanesque or Happy-Family-like names, the role-appropriateness of which would never be allowed of the names of characters in crime novels. One thinks of Mr Sherlock, the serendipitous Nemesis in the first Brighton Trunk Case; of Mr Death, the holder of the vital clue in the Müller case; of Chief Superintendent Proven Sharpe, the solver of several English West Country cases; of –

The three association-names are sufficent as provers of the point; a long list would only be handy for a game of Trivial Pursuit for keen readers of murder stories. But such a list would be deficient without the name of the elderly doctor who refused to give it to the reporter for the *Times*. He was a Cook (Roland of that ilk) – and of the too many extra-investigative cooks in the Elwell case, he meddled most influentially.

Considering his refrain, it is understandable why he

---

1. Harrap, London, 1987; St Martin's Press, New York, 1988.

preferred to remain anonymous. Supposing that he was not an egomaniac, even any of those would have shown a certain shyness if they had had the temerity to say what he said, which was this:

Charles Norris [the Chief Medical Examiner of New York City] ought to be sacked for having failed to do the most important thing that should have been done at the autopsy, *viz* the photographing of Elwell's eyeballs — for it was a well-known fact that dead retinas retained photographic images of the last thing they jointly saw. Dr Norris needn't have taken a photograph of the photographs if Elwell had been shot from behind; but as Elwell had been shot by someone in his full view, a pair of pictures of the murderer had been available for anyone with a camera suited to taking snaps of dead eyeballs to photograph, having remembered to load the camera with ultra-sensitive film that, when developed by an ultra-sensitive developer, would reveal what the retinas had retained. There might still be time to remedy Dr Norris's sin of omission. The body should be exhumed — at dead of night would be best, since there was no telling whether or not eyeballs grown accustomed to the darkness within a coffin had their images wiped out by unexpected light.

All but one of the reporters who did stints in West Seventieth Street wished that the oracular Dr Cook would go away — or, better still, bequeath his eyeballs to researchers at Bellevue Hospital, and instantly drop dead. The reporter who had no such wish worked for the *Times*. Presumably he was not the crowd-counting one. Whichever of them he was, he seems to have visited his newspaper's morgue, looked in the drawer marked E for Eyeballs, and there found a cutting that suggested that someone in the *Sûreté*, unrelated to Jules Verne, had, if the translator had got it right, commented on the *possibility* of what Dr Cook was broadcasting as ophthalmic fact to visitors to West Seventieth Street, however many of them there were. Consequently, the *Times* published an article, 'How Paris Would Treat the Elwell Case', that contained implicit criticism of Dr Norris for having neglected to photograph, stare into, or even lift the lids of Elwell's all-revealing eyes.

The day after the article appeared, John Dooling [an assistant district attorney who had jumped on the Elwell publicity bandwagon] was placed in an awkward position by yet another of the *Times* reporters, who, catching him in the presence of detectives, asked him to comment on the article. Not wishing to speak ill of the produce of a journalist – particularly not of anything by a journalist employed by the *Times* – Dooling temporised, muttering uncomplimentarily about the French police but raising his voice to say that the account of their methods had interested him 'very much'. So grown in confidence as to be willing to admit that he didn't know everything, he said that he knew nothing about the retina-retention notion.

A detective butted in: 'That is a pure invention of fiction – an absurdity of short-story writers.'

Shocked by such heresy against the press, Dooling sought to distance himself from it. 'Well, I am going to find out about the theory,' he announced. 'I will speak to expert photographers and medical men on that subject.' Turning to Captain Carey [the leader of one of the investigative groups], he asked if Elwell's eyes had been photographed –

'and the Captain only smiled.'

Dr Norris, when quizzed by reporters, put Carey's smile into angry words, saying that even if the notion held water, which it didn't, it was irrelevant to the Elwell case: Elwell had not died for some time after being shot, and, while lingering, may have opened his eyes, and must have *had* them opened – by the ambulance surgeon or by a hospital nurse or intern, or by all of them; and perhaps others. So if there had been any 'last image' on his retinas, it would not have been of his murderer but of one or more ministering angels.

In the original publishings of the above, there is a footnote. Here it is, made an addendum:

The eyes are – or, at any rate, used to be – favoured secondary targets of gunmen employed by Mafiosi to 'wipe out' people deemed to be offensive; but that may have had a *pour encourager les autres* inspiration as opposed to a superstitious self-protective one.

Acknowledgements and Sources

Other than those given in the text: 'A Slaying on Saint Valentine's Day', 'The Widow of Hardscrabble', 'The Well and the Dream' and 'An Astrological Postscript' are published by permission of the respective authors. 'Calling Madame Isherwood . . .' was first published in *Vanity Fair* (USA), June 1928. 'A Surfeit of Spirits', which first appeared, slightly shorter, in *Master Detective*, is published by permission of the compiler. 'Amityville Revisited' is published by permission of the author. 'The Ghost of Sergeant Davies', from *Twelve Scots Trials* (Green, Edinburgh, 1913), is published by permission of Mrs Marjorie Roughead. 'Devils in the Flesh', from *The Sex War and Others* (Owen, London, 1973), is published by permission of Mrs Margaret Heppenstall. 'The Hand of God or Somebody', parts of which first appeared in *The Black Museum* (by Jonathan Goodman and Bill Waddell [Curator]; Harrap, London, 1987), is published by permission of the author. 'The Gutteridge Murder' is from Volume II of *Crime and Its Detection* (Gresham, London, 1931).